THE SINEWS OF SCRIPTURE

A Handbook on Biblical Genealogies

STEPHEN C. SHAFFER

PENIEL PRESS

THE SINEWS OF SCRIPTURE

Copyright © 2024 by Stephen C. Shaffer

All rights reserved.

No part of this book may be reproduced in any form or by any electronic or mechanical means, including information storage and retrieval systems, without written permission from the author, except for the use of brief quotations in a book review.

All Scripture quotations, unless otherwise indicated, are taken from the New Revised Standard Version Bible (NRSV), copyright © 1989 National Council of the Churches of Christ in the United States of America. Used by permission. All rights reserved worldwide.

Scripture citations marked (NIV) are taken from the Holy Bible, New International Version, NIV. Copyright ©1973, 1978, 1984, 2011 by Biblica, Inc. Used by permission of Zondervan. All rights reserved worldwide. www.zondervan.com The NIV and New International Version are trademarks registered in the United States Patent and Trademark Office by Biblica, Inc.

>Peniel Press
>43 Stowe Terrace Brantford, ON N3T 6P2 Canada
>www.penielpress.com

Cover design by Olga Shaffer
Cover background image by Brenda Clarke (Texture/Background 11)

PAPERBACK ISBN: 978-1-7779787-9-2
EBOOK ISBN: 978-1-0688675-0-7

For Dad,
the keeper of the family stories

Contents

Introduction	vii
The Purpose of Genealogies	1
How to Read the Bible: *An Overview*	13
Spreading & Reversing the Curse: *Genesis 4-5*	26
Expansion & Narrowing Genealogies: *Genesis 10-11*	38
The Pattern of Patience: *Genesis 25*	50
The Ghosts of Esau: *Genesis 36*	62
Family Blessings: *Genesis 46, 48-49*	77
Radical Faith & Ordinary Faithfulness: *Ruth 4*	92
Breathing with Both Lungs: *Matthew 1:1-18*	99
Reading Backwards: *Luke 3:23-38*	115
Conclusion: *Three Key Questions for Every Genealogy*	127
For Further Reading	132
Acknowledgements	135

Introduction

This book was born out of four years preaching through the book of Genesis. In two separate sermon series at the Reformed Church of Stout, I preached through Genesis 1-11 and Genesis 12-23. After moving to Brantford, Ontario, I spent two summers preaching through Genesis 24-36 and 37-50 at Bethel Reformed Church. Preaching through Genesis means encountering a lot of genealogies. At first, I struggled to find any purpose or meaning in these difficult passages. However, I refused to skip over them and the more I dove into the genealogies, the more fascinating and exciting they became.

Part of my sermon process is to memorize the Scripture passage. Through memorizing, I become intimately familiar with all the nooks and crannies of these passages, the seemingly odd details that are sweet in my mouth but bitter in my stomach. Memorizing for over ten years changed my relationship with the Bible and helped me notice connections across Scripture in the smallest of phrases. This commitment to the smallest details of the Bible impacted my preaching and my reading of this passages. When coupled with a conviction to show forth the gospel from every passage, the genealogies came alive.

However, after each sermon, I would receive similar comments: "Pastor, I don't know how you always get something out of a genealogy. *I* could never do that." Friend, I think you can. The more I studied, the more I realized that there was nothing particularly special or technical about what I was doing. Most of how I read the genealogies did not require any extra expertise, just a certain kind of attention and vision. It is more art than science.

There is value in technical expertise. We need books that use extensive language and cultural study. I have personally benefited from many of these books and there will be a list in the back with resources for those who want to read further. Yet, most Christians I encounter feel disempowered to read the Bible if they think they *need* such expertise to read the Bible well. So I set out to write something ordinary Christians can use to increase their confidence and focus their attention as they read the biblical genealogies. "All Scripture is God-breathed and is useful for teaching, reproof, correction, and training in righteousness" (2 Tim 3:16). That includes biblical genealogies.

The Sinews of Scripture is my attempt to lay out a way of reading the genealogies of the Bible that is useful for building up our faith. The opening chapter provides a broad framework for understanding genealogies by laying out three main purposes why God included them in the Bible: family story, the search for the child, and the sinews of Scripture. The second chapter gives an overview of my basic method of reading the Bible, which applies beyond reading genealogies. It answers three questions: What is the Bible?, What is it for?, and How do we read it? The

Introduction

following eight chapters look at different passages in the Bible that contain biblical genealogies as examples of how to read them in a way that is useful for teaching, reproof, correction, and training in righteousness. These chapters engage all the genealogies of Genesis as well those found in Ruth, Matthew, and Luke. The book concludes with a summary of what we learned, as well as three starting questions that can be asked of any biblical genealogy.

I won't promise that if you read this book you will suddenly find joy in every biblical genealogy. My hope and prayer is simply that we will learn not to skim through them, but to slow down and hear all that God is saying to us.

— Stephen C. Shaffer

March 14, 2024
Brantford, Ontario

THE PURPOSE OF GENEALOGIES

Genealogies are the connective tissue of the Bible.

Have you ever tried to read all the way through the Bible and feel like you hit a pothole? You are driving along through the story of Scripture and then, *clunk*, you hit a genealogy listing all sorts of names you have trouble pronouncing and never see again in the Bible. Some of us plough through it, hoping to get to the good stuff later. Others pull over the side of the road and get out of the car. We give up trying to read, because we don't know what to do with what we read.

What if I told you that the genealogies in the Bible did not have to be a pothole on the road of reading? What if, instead, they could be a place to pause and see the whole Bible more clearly? The genealogies of the Bible are the sinews of Scripture, the connective tissue God uses to hold together the various parts of the Bible and connect them together into a coherent whole. As 2 Timothy 3:16 says, "All Scripture is God-breathed and is useful for teaching, reproof, correction, and training in righteousness." "All

Scripture" includes the genealogies. They are *useful*. God placed them in the Bible for a purpose. In this chapter, we will examine three different reasons for the frequency of biblical genealogies before exploring our driving image for the place of genealogies in the Bible: they are the sinews of Scripture.

A FAMILY STORY

First, genealogies remind us that the Bible is a family story. According to my family history, our Irish ancestors, the Carneys, came to the United States on a boat during the Irish Potato Famine. Even though I clearly do not remember those events (nor does anyone alive in my family), whenever I read about the Irish Potato Famine, I feel connected to the story. These are not random historical events — my family experienced the hunger, the fear, and the displacement of the famine. Another one of my ancestors fought against Napoleon in the Battle of Waterloo and distinguished himself in such a way that the King granted him land near Montreal. I cannot read about the Napoleonic Wars without feeling connected in some way, even though I have never been anywhere near Waterloo. The story involves my family and so it becomes more personal. This is *family* history. We have family books with genealogies containing names that I don't recognize, but they are *my* people, even if I never met them.

In a similar way, the genealogies are important in the Bible because this is family history. The Bible deals with individuals and nations, but always within the contexts of larger families. The twelve tribes of Israel were originally twelve brothers (Gen. 35:23-26). The nations of Edom and Israel were originally twins – Jacob and Esau (Gen. 25:23-26). Egypt comes from one of the sons of Ham (Gen. 10:6).

The Purpose of Genealogies

The Bible is not simply dealing with ancient geo-politics, but with the joy and drama of family.

In the same way that knowing my family history helps me feel more connected to the events of the past, the genealogies can open us up to be more connected to the stories of the Bible. This was particularly true for Israel. For generation upon generation, these stories were told. Stories of faithfulness and unfaithfulness, of victory and defeat, of joy and trial. Yet, intermixed with these stories were genealogies. These genealogies contained name after name that may be unfamiliar to many of us, but would have sparked joy in the hearts of the Israelites.

When the sons and families of Benjamin were named in Genesis, the people of the tribe of Benjamin would have each listened and waited to hear the name of their ancestor. "The children of Benjamin: Bela, Becher, Ashbel, Gera, Naaman, Ehi, Rosh, Muppim, Huppim, and Ard" (Gen 46:21). Some gathered were descendants of Gera and others of Ehi, but they would have known and felt themselves connected to the story. The story of Joseph and his brothers was not just some isolated story from the past, it was *their* story.

When the sons of Judah read 1 Chronicles, they would have waited to hear of their part of the family. When 1 Chronicles 1:28 was read ("The sons of Onan: Shammai and Jada. The sons of Shammai: Nadab and Abishur"), we can almost imagine a little boy leaning over to the child next to him and whispering, "I'm from the family of Abishur" and the boy whispering back, "Well, I'm from Nadab! We are practically cousins!" The genealogies connected them to the story of God's work among his people, as well as to one another. They saw not only themselves, but each other as being part of the biblical story.

The same was true for those returning from exile. The opening genealogical list in Ezra would have placed their family in the story of Scripture. Whether or not they knew each of the names on the list, they would certainly have known where *they* connected to the story, where *they* belonged. In a similar way, when I read my family genealogical books going back a couple hundred years I do not know most of the names there, but I certainly know *my* ancestors.

One of the chief reasons that God placed these genealogies in the pages of Scripture was so that his people would see this story as *their* story. They belonged to the people and family of God. What took place long ago matters for who they are and who they are called to be. This connection was particularly important for the people of Israel, as they carried the promises and covenant of God. They needed to know intimately that they were part of *this* people, that the promises, the commands, and the calling were all for them.

As spiritual children of Abraham, Christians are adopted into the great family of God. We may not be able to name our direct biological ancestors in these stories or find our distant grand-father in the genealogies, but these stories are not just isolated incidents from the historical past, but family stories. In Jesus, we become part of the family of God. The genealogies remind us that these stories are family stories, which means they are for us as well.

THE BIRTH OF THE SON

The second reason so many genealogies are included in the Bible is that the drama of Scripture centers around the promise of a child. From the moment sin entered into the world, all of creation has been waiting for the birth of the

The Purpose of Genealogies

Son.

God created the world and everything in it. He made the sun and moon, the grass and trees, the fish and birds. He also made a man and a woman to bear his image and to rule over creation under his rule (Gen. 1:27-28). However, our first parents trusted the wicked serpent over God. They ate fruit from the one tree from which God had commanded them not to eat (Gen. 3:1-7). Their eyes were opened, they realized they were naked, and they hid. When God called them out of their hiding and all was revealed, God pronounced judgment upon the man, the woman, and the snake. Yet, contained in the judgment on the snake was a promise: "I will put enmity between you and the woman, and between your offspring and hers; he will strike your head and you will strike his heel" (Gen. 3:15). This promise came to be known as the "proto-evangelium," that is the "original gospel." God promised that there would be an offspring of Eve, a son, who would crush the head of the serpent. Though this Son's heel would be struck, the serpent would be defeated. This is the first promise that there would be good news on the other side of sin, that God would one day send a deliverer.

Ever since that moment, with every birth of every child, there is hidden the question, "Is this child the one?" When Cain kills Abel, there must be another line through which this child would be born (Gen. 4:25). Seth's lineage is traced to Noah and the flood (Gen. 5). Each child is born, but is not *the* child. After the flood, two of the sons of Noah are separated from the promise and the story follows the children of Shem, who bears the hope that one of his children would be the one (Gen. 10-11). Eventually God calls Abram and Sarai and promises them children. God makes a covenant with Abram, renames him Abraham, and promises that through Abraham and his offspring all the nations would be blessed. The next several generations contain the struggle to have children. Will the child actually be born or will the promise die out? Sarai struggles with barrenness (Gen. 16:1, 17:17-22). Rebekah struggles to have children (Gen. 25:21). Leah has children, but Rachel struggles and eventually dies in childbirth (Gen. 29:31-30:24, 35:16-18). Over and over again, the question lingers. Is this the child? As the struggle for children continues, the promise of God seems to hang in the balance.

Yet, God remains faithful. The birth of children and the tracing of families becomes so important in the Bible because it is all part of the anticipation of the Messiah, Jesus Christ, the perfect son of Eve who will redeem us and set things right. The Bible contains so many genealogies because the whole Bible is longing for Christ. It is no accident that both the gospel of Matthew and the gospel of Luke contain long genealogies of Jesus in their opening chapters. We will explore those genealogies in detail in a later chapter, but their placement at the forefront of the gospels makes sense when we remember the promise of Genesis 3:15. A son would come, the Son of Eve, to crush the serpent. All of creation and, indeed, all of Scripture has been awaiting his coming.

The descriptions of the reigns of kings in 1-2 Kings and 1-2 Chronicles follow a similar pattern. These kings — their deeds and misdeeds — are recorded not just because the facts are interesting, but because the question remains, "Is this the true king? The true heir of David that God promised would reign forever?" (2 Samuel 7:4-16). In fact, the Bible makes it clear that if we simply want more information, we can look elsewhere, in the Books of the Annals of the Kings of Israel and Judah (e.g. 1 Kings 15:23, 31). Each king (the

The Purpose of Genealogies

most righteous and the most wicked) falls short of being the true son of David. Even in failure, they point ahead to the true King who would one day come, Jesus Christ.

The lists of sons in the genealogies makes sense in the Bible when we remember how all Scripture points ahead to Jesus Christ. The lists of kings makes sense for a similar reason: all of them point ahead to Jesus. "Then beginning with Moses and all the prophets, he [Jesus] interpreted to them the things about himself in all the scriptures" (Luke 24:27) The "things about Jesus in all the scriptures" includes the genealogies. The Holy Spirit included them in the pages of Holy Scripture because they point to Jesus Christ.

Connecting Past, Present, and Future Together

However, there is one final reason the Bible includes so many genealogies — one that I believe is most significant for us reading today. The genealogies connect the Bible together — past, present, and future. The various portions of Scripture are drawn and held together by the genealogies. For this reason, genealogies should not sit at the margins of our Bible reading, but are vital for understanding how the whole Bible fits together.

Connecting to the Past: Genealogies help bridge the gaps between various eras of the biblical story. The genealogy of Genesis 5 connects the narrative of creation and fall – of Adam, Eve, Cain, and Abel – to the story of Noah and the flood. It serves as a bridge between the two, connecting the Biblical past to the Biblical present. Genesis 10 does the same when it connects Noah and the flood to Babel and Abram. The genealogies of Jesus in Matthew and Luke serve to create a deep connection between the Old and New Testaments. These genealogies hold the two testaments together as one book.

These connections to the past can also help us interpret the Bible in new and fresh ways. The genealogy of Esau connects him to Saul and Lot, which helps us better understand all three. The genealogy of Jesus includes four women (Rahab, Ruth, Tamar, and Bathsheba), which helps us better understand those women and Jesus. It is part of the burden of the rest of this book to demonstrate how seeing these connections in the genealogies will enable us to read the whole of the Bible more profitably.

Shadows of the Future: Genealogies also provide interpretive context for understanding later stories in the Bible. In many of the early genealogies we are told the ancestors who would give rise to entire nations and peoples: the Moabites and Ammonites result from Lot's incestuous union with his daughters (Gen 19:37-38). Both the Egyptians and the Canaanites comes from Ham, who was cursed by Noah for looking upon his father's nakedness (Gen 10:6). Jacob and Esau – both in their birth and in their genealogy – foreshadow a contrast and conflict that will carry on throughout the biblical story (Gen. 25:19-34). Jacob's blessings on his sons foreshadow their later actions and character (Gen. 48-49). The genealogy of Ruth tells us we should see this struggle for a child in the context of the future birth of David.

The genealogies not only connect backward to the stories and people who have come before, but stretch forward to connect to what has not yet come to pass in the biblical narrative.

Interpreting the Present: In connecting past and future, the genealogies help us understand the very stories these genealogies are embedded in and the people mentioned therein. We not only read Ruth in light of David, but David in light of Ruth. We not only read Judah and Tamar in light of the genealogies of Judah, but in light of her inclusion in the genealogies of Jesus. Understanding the connections between Saul, Lot, and Esau in Esau's genealogy will shed light on the character of Esau and his place within the biblical drama.

The genealogies in the Bible have drawn generations of readers — including the spiritual children of Abraham — into the family story of the Bible. These stories are not simply history that happened long ago, but they are *our* story. The genealogies also touch upon the great drama of the whole Bible, the search for the child of Eve who will crush the head of the serpent. But the genealogies also help us more deeply understand the biblical story itself by connecting what came before to what comes after in order to gain a fuller grasp of the whole of Scripture.

THE SINEWS OF SCRIPTURE

In order for us to walk, we need our muscles to work. Muscles are the organs that pull and enable us to move. As an infant learns to stand or to walk, we can see the muscles developing and strengthening for this purpose. Without muscles, we cannot walk.

In order for us to walk, we also need bones. The bones give us the stability and structure to be able to move. The muscles in our legs, feet, back, and chest pull on the bones in our body to help us move. The muscles provide the strength and the bones the structure. The muscles provide the action, but movement happens when they pull upon our bones and move them. A body without bones would struggle to move for there would be nothing for the muscles to pull on.

However, there is another thing needed for us to be able

to walk: connective tissue. Muscles and bones might be necessary for us to walk, but we need something that connects the muscle to the bone, bones to other bones, and muscles to other muscles. We need sinews and ligaments that bind together all our bones and muscles so that we can walk, dance, run, and leap. Without these sinews, the body would fall apart. It would just be a collection of bones and muscles, but be unable to move.

The genealogies are the connective tissue of the Bible. Their purpose is to hold the Scriptures together, to forge connections such that the story of the Bible is a coherent and connected whole. They are an instrument in the hand of the Spirit to transform the Bible from a collection of short stories, teachings, songs, and letters, into a unified whole. The narratives might be like the muscles that pull the story of Scripture forward. The law and the letters might be like the bones that give us structure and stability. But without the genealogies holding the whole together, it can become easy for us to see each book of the Bible or even each chapter or verse within a book as a separate and unrelated entity. By connecting past, present, and future together, the genealogies help us see the Bible as a whole book. Our sinews and ligaments help connect our muscles and bones so we can walk. The genealogies, the sinews of Scripture, help us be able to walk as disciples of Jesus.

Genealogies are not the only instrument the Spirit uses to unify Scripture, but this is part of the Spirit's purpose in including them in the Bible.

Conclusion

In this book, we hope to convince you that the biblical genealogies are not potholes on the road of reading the Bible. Instead, they are the sinews of Scripture, the

The Purpose of Genealogies

connective tissue God uses to hold the Bible together as a coherent whole. The genealogies have been included in the Bible for at least three reasons. First, the Bible is a family story. Tracing the family tree reminds us and invites us into the story. Second, from the moment we exited Eden, we have been waiting for the promised child of Eve who would save. Every birth recorded, every son born, is an echo of that promise until the birth of the Son. There are no genealogies in the Bible after the birth of Jesus. His birth is the fulfillment of all the genealogies of the Bible. Lastly, the genealogies connect the past, present, and future together, so that we can see the various parts and characters of Scripture in light of one another.

It is this last purpose that will drive the rest of this book. We will look at eight different genealogies in the Bible as examples to help us learn better how to read all of the genealogies. Our hope is that working through these examples will transform how you read, not only the genealogies, but the whole of Scripture. Our hope is that you will read it more joyfully, more faithfully, more humbly, and more confidently.

But before we move into the genealogies itself, we need to explain our basic approach to reading the Bible.

Discussion Questions:

1. How have you experienced reading the genealogies in the Bible in the past? What are you hoping might change from reading this book?

2. How does your family keep its genealogy? What interesting stories (good or bad) do you know about your family's past?

3. How do the genealogies point to Jesus? How might this change what you are looking for when reading the genealogies?

4. Which parts of the Bible seem most closely connected for you? Which seem most disconnected? How would it impact your faith to see all of the Bible connected together?

How to Read the Bible:

An Overview

Not one letter, not one stroke of a letter, will pass from the Law until all is accomplished. – Matthew 5:18

While this book is about biblical genealogies, it is really about how to read the Bible. Our goal is to grow to understand biblical genealogies, so that we become better readers of Scripture as a whole. So before diving into the genealogies, we should take a step back and look at how to read the Bible by asking three important questions: "What is the Bible?", "What is the Bible for?," and, only then, "How do we read the Bible?" How we answer each of these questions will go a long way to determining how we approach the Bible in general and the genealogies in particular.

What is the Bible?

The Bible is the very Word of God, the means by which God reveals himself. Drilling down a bit deeper, we can identify and defend specific properties of the Bible that shape how we read and understand it. Every theologian has a slightly different list of properties and may use slightly different terms, but they largely fall into four categories.

First, there is the *truth, certainty, and infallibility* of Scripture. Scripture reveals God truly and reliably. The seventeenth century Dutch theologian, Petrus van Mastricht, sums up our position nicely: "This general truth [about Scripture] implies certain specifics: its doctrinal and historical statements are most accurately consistent with the matter and the facts; its practical statements with the will of God; its prophecies, promises, and threats with the future event – no differently and no less than if they had been eyewitness testimonies. And that is the case because it has the God of truth as its author; Christ as the very truth it contains, and as its faithful witness; and the Holy Spirit, truth's infallible inspirer, as its guide."[1] In van Mastricht's time and ours, there are differences about how to handle more thorny issues in the Bible, but the initial assumption should always be that the Bible is a true and reliable witness.

Second, there is the *purity, holiness, perfection, and sufficiency* of Scripture. The Belgic Confession, Article 7 says that, "We believe that this Holy Scripture contains the will of God completely and that everything one must believe to be saved is sufficiently taught in it."[2] We can know true things about God in Creation (known as the "Book of Nature"), but it is only through the Book of Scripture that we come to know salvation in Jesus Christ. When it comes

---

[1] Petrus van Mastricht, *Theoretical-Practical Theology, Volume 1: Prolegomena*, trans. Todd M. Rester, ed. Joel R. Beeke (Grand Rapids, MI: Reformation Heritage Books, 2018), 127.
[2] Belgic Confession, Article 7, from *Our Faith: Ecumenical Creeds, Reformed Confessions, and Other Resources* (Grand Rapids, MI: Faith Alive, 2013).

to knowing who God is, what he has done, and who God has made us to be, God's Word is a sufficient source of that knowledge. Anywhere else we look will be insufficient for true knowledge of God. If the first property says the Bible is *reliable*, this one says the Bible is *enough*. It is holy and lacks nothing that we need for life and salvation. As John Calvin says, "it is better to limp along this path than to dash with all speed outside it."[3] The 'enough'-ness of the Bible does not mean we do not engage with tradition, or logic, or experience. But we never consider these as separate or independent sources of knowledge of God. Reason, tradition, and experience can, at times, be helpful guides, but it is never Scripture & Reason, Scripture & Tradition, or Scripture & Experience that forms our basis of knowledge of God and ourselves. This is what was meant by the Reformation slogan, *sola scriptura* ("Scripture alone"). Scripture alone is sufficient for knowing God and his salvation.

Third, there is the *perspicuity or efficacy* of Scripture. A less used, but perhaps better term is *clarity*. I like what Herman Bavinck says here, "Scripture speaks in the language of life, of the heart, of immediacy, of inspiration, and is thus understandable for every man, going forth into every generation, never growing old in its time, and therefore classic in the highest sense, in an utterly unique sense of the word."[4] Scripture is effective in accomplishing God's purposes for it. The Lord says, "As the rain and the snow come down from heaven, and do not return to it without watering the earth and making it bud and flourish,

---

[3] John Calvin, *The Institutes of Christian Religion*, trans. Ford Lewis Battles, ed. John T. McNeill (Philadelphia: Westminster Press, 1960), 1.VI.3.

[4] Herman Bavinck, *On Preaching & Preachers*, trans. & ed. James P. Eglinton (Peabody, Mass.: Hendrickson Publishers, 2017), 37-38.

so that it yields seed for the sower and bread for the eater, *so is my word that goes out from my mouth*: It will not return to me empty, but *will accomplish what I desire* and achieve the purpose for which I sent it." (Isaiah 55:10-11, italics for emphasis). Scripture is effective and clear, that is, it is able to be understood.

Understanding Scripture is not limited to the educated and the elite. This is one of the reasons that we will not be directly appealing to the original languages or archaeological discoveries in this book. One way people can read the genealogies profitably is to work to understand the meaning of the names and even make connections to the archaeological record. There is much to gain from that method (and I have personally been enriched by it), but we want to present a method that can be used by those without specialized knowledge. When our methods of reading Scripture, particularly the hard passages, depend too much upon specialized linguistic knowledge, then we undermine the confidence of Christians to be able to read the Bible. This is not a critique of expertise at all, but I am setting aside this valuable discipline in order to ask "What would help my mother's bible study to read these genealogies profitably?" How can we read the Bible well in such a way that demonstrates our trust in its clarity?

For the Bible is not a labyrinth that can only be navigated by specialists, but is the clear thread that leads us out of the confusing labyrinths of our (mis)understandings of God. The image of Scripture as the thread leading us out of the labyrinth comes from John Calvin: "For we should so reason that the splendor of the divine countenance, which even the apostle calls "unapproachable" is for us like an inexplicable labyrinth unless we are conducted into it by the thread of the Word; so that it is better to limp along this path than to dash with all speed outside it."[5] Calvin is drawing the picture from the story of Theseus in Greek Mythology. The hero Theseus was placed in a labyrinth with a Minotaur. The labyrinth was dark and complicated and created so no one should be able to get out. However, the princess Ariadne gave Theseus a ball of red thread that he unrolled as he walked through the labyrinth. After killing the Minotaur, Theseus was able to follow the thread back and find his way out. For Calvin, left to ourselves, our knowledge of God is like a labyrinth. It is full of twists and turns, truth and error, and something we can never escape on our own. By our own wit or wisdom, we cannot come to know God truly. God's "countenance" (or face) is "unapproachable." In our sin we will constantly twist any truth about God into something else. It is only if we are given a thread, the Word of God, will we be lead out of the labyrinth into true knowledge of God. In addition to the labyrinth, Calvin also talks about a man limping and running. It is better to limp along according to God's Word than to run apart from it. It is not about the speed at which you move, but whether you are moving according to God's Word, according to the only means provided for you to come to God. Why is Scripture the only means? Because it holds forth Jesus Christ, our Redeemer, the Way, the Truth, and the Life. So even if you are limping in the Word, that is much better than to run with all your might anywhere else.

While we value education and the use of original languages and grammar in studying the Bible, we also believe that the truth of Scripture is fundamentally clear and not hidden. The Bible's message is simple and clear enough for a child to understand, but deep enough that scholars can spend a lifetime studying it. This property

---
[5] Calvin, *Institutes*, 1.VI.3

guards against the Bible being metaphorically taken out of the hands of the people and kept only in the hands of pastors and professors.

Fourth, there is the *authority* of Scripture. We see this in Belgic Confession, Article 5, where the books of the Bible are received "for the regulating, founding, and establishing of our faith."[6] The content of our faith and shape of our life as disciples is ruled by the Word of God. It is the norm, the standard, for our faith and life as Christians. We are governed, not by the whims of culture or our feelings or our desires, but by God's Word. For Christians, Scripture is also the *final* authority, the final court of appeals, so to speak, in any controversy on what we believe or how we live. In practical terms, if I read God's Word and, through study, I am confident that I understand it correctly, but I still don't like what it says, then the problem is with me and not with the Word of God. That's one way that this authority of Scripture can function.

The first question that shapes how we interpret the Bible is "What is it?" We typically identify certain properties of Scripture that make a difference in how we read the Bible. I grouped them in four categories: the *reliability* of Scripture, the *sufficiency* of Scripture, the *clarity* of Scripture, and the *authority* of Scripture. The second question we must answer before we can get to the practical dimension of how to read the Bible is this: What is it for?

What is the Bible for?

Purpose determines use. We use a wrench to turn bolts, not to hammer in nails because we know what it is for. When someone hands me some chocolate and tells me that it is for my children, I now know what to do with the

---
[6] Belgic Confession, Article 5.

chocolate. I don't eat it myself, even if that seems like fun. I relate to it based upon the purpose for which it was given. In a similar way, knowing why Scripture was given will shape how we read it, relate to it, and what we do with it. What is the Bible for? According to the Belgic Confession, the Scriptures were given "with special care for us and for our salvation."[7]

Scripture was given "for us." By "us," we mean the church. Scripture was given to build up the church and to glorify God. When John Calvin argued for the Bible to be translated into the language of the common people, he used the image of the church as the school of Christ. The Bible should be in the hands of the people, in a language they can understand, so that we would grow in our ability to encourage and correct one another in the faith and thus grow as a church.[8] The natural home of the Bible is the church. God's Word is also an apologetic and evangelistic word, but its primary place is in the life of the church.

Scripture was also given "for our salvation." John 20:31 says "But these are written that you may believe that Jesus is the Messiah, the Son of God, and that by believing you may have life in his name." Scripture was given to be received *by* faith in Christ and Scripture was given *for* faith in Christ. This includes knowledge of God and communion with God. It involves repentance, faith, and trust in Jesus Christ. There is much to be learned through the Bible, but its primary purpose is that we might cling to Christ in faith. This purpose defines what we expect to find in the Bible.

---

[7] Belgic Confession, Article 3.
[8] Randall Zachman, "Learning to Read Scripture for Ourselves: The Guidance of Erasmus, Luther, and Calvin" in *The People's Book: The Reformation and the Bible*, eds. Jennifer Powell McNutt & David Lauber (Downer's Grove, IL: Intervarsity Press, 2017), 64-68.

How to read it?

With the properties and purpose of the Bible in place, how do we actually read it well? There is a basic pattern of reading that we might call Whole-Part-Whole.

Step 1: Focus on the Whole

First, begin with prayer. Christian devotion and prayer are not casual add-ons to the process of reading the Bible, but absolutely central. Prayers for the work of the Holy Spirit and a vibrant life of Christian devotion and prayer are crucial for reading the Bible. The idea of being a "dispassionate observer" or trying to get objective distance is not a properly Christian way of reading the Bible. In short, trying to set aside prayer and Christian faith before reading the Bible is not reading the Bible *as* God's Word. Instead, reading the Bible as God's Word begins with prayer and faith in Christ.

Second, consult the tradition of interpreters as a guide, not an authority. We are never the first to read any passage of Scripture. We don't need to pretend to be. The sufficiency and clarity of Scripture does not mean that we never read any other books or that we cannot learn much from the reading of others. However, this great tradition of interpretation functions as a guide, not an authority. They are like wise elders we do well to listen to, but do not always agree with. John Calvin's commentaries are a good example of this. He regularly interacts with Augustine and Chrysostom's interpretation of a given passage. Sometimes he agrees with them, sometimes he disagrees, but he always listens and gives their interpretation respect.

Third, we assume the overall unity and coherence of Scripture. There are sixty-six different books in the Bible. Each author, under the inspiration of the Holy Spirit, writes differently, in a different context, and to a different original audience. Yet, because the ultimate author of Scripture is God and God does not contradict Himself, the Bible is fundamentally coherent. The unity and coherence of Scripture is crucial for how we will read the genealogies. The genealogies of Genesis not only tell us something about what is going on in the book of Genesis, but they can be set alongside genealogies in Matthew and Luke because the same Spirit inspired, shaped, and preserved both passages. Are there sometimes tensions between portions of the Bible? Yes. Are there contradictions? No. There are differences in different eras of salvation history – particularly between the Old and New Testaments – but there is a fundamental unity of God's Word. This unity shapes the process of using clear passages in Scripture to interpret more difficult ones, even if they are in a totally different part of the Bible. You can only do this if you believe in a fundamental unity of God's Word, that it speaks with one voice – God's.

Step 2: Pay attention to the Part

Next, we move from the whole to the part, the particular passage of Scripture you are studying. In looking at a particular passage of Scripture, there is great value in paying attention to the words in the original languages and the grammar of Greek, Hebrew, and Aramaic. Christians have frequently written word books, grammars, and dictionaries to help in the reading of Scripture. This volume will not focus on that particular work, but only the fruit of that work in English translations readily accessible to everyday Christians. Jesus tells us that not a stroke of a letter will pass away from the Law until all is accomplished (Mt 5:18). Every word and phrase in the Bible is there for a reason. Especially in a time where producing and preserving texts was extremely expensive, the fact that God preserved these details should force us to pay attention and contemplate them.

So in a particular passage, we look at language and context, focusing on the plain sense of the text. Often "plain sense" is equivalent to what is commonly called the "literal meaning" or "the intent of the author," but not always. Because the Bible is a coherent whole whose fundamental author is God, there are times where the literal meaning of a passage is not strictly a historical meaning, but a theological or Christological one. Sometimes the plain sense is the spiritual sense. We can sometimes draw together the literal and spiritual meanings of the text.[9] In short, when it comes to approaching the individual passage, we focus on reading a text in its literary, canonical, and theological context.

Step 3: Connect back to the Whole

Lastly, we move back to consider the whole by interpreting Scripture in light of other Scripture. This is the "canonical context," since we read Scripture in light of the whole canon – the entire Bible. It is here that we will most clearly see how the genealogies connect the past, present, and future. Having looked closely at the details of the genealogies and worked to get clear on their meaning, we will look at other places in the Bible where the same (or similar) events have happened or words have been used. Repetition in the Bible is God's way of drawing attention to something and creating connections. For example, Genesis 49 tells of the blessings on the sons of Israel. Concerning

---
[9] Craig G. Bartholomew, *Introducing Biblical Hermeneutics: A Comprehensive Framework for Hearing God in Scripture* (Grand Rapids, MI: Baker Academic, 2015), 198.

Judah it says, "binding his foal to the vine, his donkey's colt to the choice vine." We should spend time trying to get the literal meaning of the text, but then ask, "where else have I seen this?" This takes us to Zechariah 9:9, "behold your king comes to you riding on a colt, the foal of a donkey" then to the triumphal entry of Jesus, where he comes in riding on a colt and foal. This question ("Where else have I seen this?") opens up the vistas of Scripture to help us see connections we would not have before. We interpret unclear passages in light of clear ones. Sometimes this means placing similar passages alongside each other, so that one clarifies the other. Other times it means placing texts that seem to be saying different things alongside each other to see what is causing the difference. Jesus tells us not to swear oaths, but Scripture frequently has godly people giving oaths or even being commanded to swear oaths by God's name. Tension, yes. Contradiction, no. So we have to interpret unclear in light of the clear, determine what is similar and what is dissimilar. This method requires an intimate knowledge of the whole body of Scripture.

When reading the Bible, there are three questions we must answer. First, what is the Bible? It is the true, sufficient, clear, and authoritative Word of God. Second, what is it for? Scripture was given for us, the church, and for our salvation. Lastly, how do we read it? We begin with the whole context of prayer, consulting the tradition, and the unity of Scripture. Then we move to the details of the passage, considering language and context to determine the plain meaning of the passage. Finally, we move to the context of Scripture as a whole, considering how this passage might be interpreted in light of the rest of the Bible.

Reading Genealogies

As we have already stated, each chapter will be unique, but the overall method will be the same. First, we will *pay attention to the details*, drilling down to the specifics of a passage and asking why God might have wanted us to know this information. Second, we will ask *Where else have I seen this?* and draw connections between the genealogy and the rest of Scripture. In reading this way, our hope is that you will grow not only in your appreciation for the genealogies of the Bible, but grow as a reader of Holy Scripture.

Discussion Questions:

1. Do you agree with the list of properties of the Bible given in this chapter? What might you add? What might you change? Which property do you believe is most important?

2. How does the reason the Bible is written change how we read it? When have you experienced how the Bible is "for you and for your salvation"?

3. Describe your normal practice of reading the Bible. Where does this chapter resonate with what you are already doing? Where does this chapter challenge your normal practice?

Spreading & Reversing the Curse:

Genesis 4-5

"100 percent of us die, and the percentage cannot be increased"
– C. S. Lewis

Genealogies are the sinews of Scripture. They serve as connective tissue that holds the story of Bible together as one coherent whole. In Genesis 4 and 5, we see the first two genealogies in the Bible. Already, these lists of generations not only cover the passage of time between Adam and Eve and the flood, but look backward to Eden and forward to the cross and resurrection of Jesus Christ. In this chapter, we will first look at the genealogy of Cain in Genesis 4 and how it shows the amplification of sin in the first several generations of humanity. Next, we will note a key repeated phrase in Genesis 5 that calls us back to the conversation between Eve and the snake in the garden. Then, we will reflect on what it means for Adam to have a son "after his own likeness." Lastly, in the birth of Noah at the end of Genesis 5, we will see how this genealogy points to Jesus Christ.

The Descendants of Cain

The first genealogy in the Bible comes on the tails of the first murder. Adam and Eve trusted the words of the serpent, ate fruit from the tree God commanded them not to eat from, and were cast from the garden. Adam and Eve then have two sons: Cain and Abel. Cain tilled the soil, while Abel kept flocks. When the two brothers brought their offerings to the Lord, God was pleased with Abel's offering, but "for Cain and his offering he had no regard" (Gen 4:5). Cain became angry and, even though the Lord warned him about his anger, Cain lured his brother out into the field and killed him. He then denied knowing anything about the incident and was marked and cursed by God.

Cain's line brings forth the beginnings of civilization. Four descendants of Cain are listed as the first to accomplish certain feats. Cain's son Enoch built a city — the first record in history (4:17). Jabal was the ancestor of those who live in tents and have livestock (4:20). Jubal was the ancestor of those who play the lyre and pipe (4:21). Tubal-cain made bronze and iron tools (4:22). From the same line springs both violence and civilization, murder and invention. This tells us that we cannot make an easy or sharp distinction between what is produced by the people of God and what is produced by the world. Since sin stains even the church, all our works will have elements of disorder in them. But since even those outside the church have been made in the image of God and retain the good gifts of creation, there can be much good found even in the cultural works of unbelievers. Cain and his descendants bring forth all sorts of violence and wickedness, but they also develop cities and husbandry.[1] They produce musical instruments and also songs of violence and revenge. They produce iron and bronze tools, but also weapons of war. God's gifts to humanity at creation are not completely erased by the fall into sin. The call to "fill the earth and subdue it" remains (Gen 1:28), as well as the power to live into this calling. Good can come even out of the twisted works of the line of Cain.

The details in Cain's genealogy remind us that we must evaluate culture — and the structures and products of culture — not merely on the basis of their origin. More important than whether something was made by a Christian or non-Christian is whether that thing is better or more fitting of God's design. God's purposes and God's kingdom, revealed in his Word, define how we evaluate such cultural artifacts as cities, music, livestock, and tools.

Reversing Cain's Legacy

However, the line of Cain brings not just culture, but violence. The very first biblical genealogy shows the spiraling of the descendants of Cain into sinful madness. Creation at the end of Genesis 2 was a paradise where Adam sang the first song, rejoicing that Eve was "bone of my bones and flesh of my flesh" (2:23). By the end of Chapter 4, creation has plunged so deeply into sin that another song was sung: "I have killed a man for wounding me, a young man for striking me. If Cain is avenged sevenfold, truly Lamech seventy-sevenfold" (4:23b-24). The sin that was lurking at Cain's door has pounced. The infection has spread down the generations and filled the human heart.

---

[1] There is also a certain irony that Cain is the ancestor of those who have livestock, when Cain tilled the soil and it was Abel who kept sheep.

Cain's line emphasizes the spread of sin after the exile from the Garden. Sin in the human heart and in human action only seems to grow as the violence of Cain escalates to the days of Lamech. The end of Cain's genealogy is the violent cursing of Lamech. Cain murdered his brother because Abel had done well. Rather than examine his own offering, he broke out in violence against his brother for the good Abel had done. Cain's descendants learned this lesson well. Minor injuries were met with extreme violence. Murder was the response to a bruise. Thankfully, this is not the end of the story of the human race. Genesis 4 already reveals that there will be a second line of children from Adam and Eve, the line of Seth. However, thankfully, Lamech's cursing is also not the end of the story of Cain. For the legacy of Cain is reversed in the teaching of Jesus:

> "You have heard that it was said to those of ancient times, 'You shall not murder'; and 'whoever murders shall be liable to judgment.' But I say to you that if you are angry with a brother or sister, you will be liable to judgment; and if you insult a brother or sister, you will be liable to the council; and if you say, 'you fool,' you will be liable to the hell of fire. So when you are offering your gift at the altar, if you remember that your brother or sister has something against you, leave your gift there before the altar and go, first be reconciled to your brother or sister and then come and offer your gift." (Mt. 5:21-24)

Offerings, anger, murder, judgment — the same elements are in the story of Cain — but instead of anger and brokenness ending in murder, Jesus calls us to end with reconciliation. In Genesis 4, Lamech learns from the legacy

of Cain and says,
> "I have killed a man for wounding me, a young man for injuring me. If Cain is avenged seven times, then Lamech seventy-seven times." (4:23b-24)

But in Matthew 18, Jesus has this conversation with Peter,
> "Then Peter came and said to him, "Lord, if another member of the church sins against me, how often should I forgive? As many as seven times?" Jesus said to him, "Not seven times, but, I tell you, seventy-seven times." (18:21-22)

Instead of a seventy-seven fold vengeance, Jesus speaks of seventy-seven fold forgiveness. The way of Christ charts a different path than that of Cain.

Parallels & Contrasts

The end of Genesis 4 already begins the transition away from the line of Cain to the line of Seth. Adam and Eve have a third son, whose birth is seen as a gift from God after Abel was murdered. This second genealogy in Genesis parallels the first. Not only does it come after the same exile from Eden and murder of Abel, but there are many shared or similar names between the two genealogies. Cain has a son named Enoch, while Seth has a son named Enosh. A later generation also has Enoch, who walked with God and was no more (4:17, 26; 5:19-24). Cain's line has Mehujael and Methushael, while Seth's has Mahalalel and Methuselah. Both lines continue until they reach a son named Lamech. The parallel names tell us that we are supposed to read them alongside each other. However, while the similarities are the first thing we might notice, this makes the contrasts more striking.

The contrasts are most vivid at the beginning and the end of these two genealogies. At the beginning of Cain's genealogy, Enoch founds a city, but at the birth of Seth people began to call upon the name of the Lord. This foreshadows what we will see later in Genesis 11, where the peoples of the earth gather together on the plain of Shinar to build a city and make a name for themselves (the Tower of Babel). Instead of humbling themselves and calling on the name of the Lord, they build a city and a tower as a way of exalting themselves. The end of the genealogies have a similar contrast: Cain's Lamech breathes out violence, while Seth's Lamech speaks words of comfort at the birth of Noah.

THE SERPENT'S LIE

Throughout the genealogy of Adam in Genesis 5, there is a consistent pattern for each named person. When so-and-so had lived a certain number of years, he became the father of such-and-such. He lived so many more years, had other sons and daughters. Altogether, he lived this many years, and then he died. Over and over again, the same pattern with the same ending: *and then he died*. Altogether, Adam, Seth, Enosh, Kenan, Mahalalel, Jared, Methuselah, Lamech lived, *and then he died*. The end of the account of the lives of these sons of Adam and Eve is a pronouncement of death.

Every one of them died. This is a reality we know too well. C.S. Lewis once said that the mortality rate for the human species hovers around 100%. In a culture that is both fascinated and terrified by death, the Bible is stark and honest. People die — rich and poor, weak and strong, faithful and faithless. The one sentence that has become universal of the human condition is "Altogether, he lived and then he died." The details are different, but the basic shape is the same — life and then death.

In the genealogy of Adam, Scripture unmasks a lie.

Where else in the Bible do we hear of death? In particular, by Genesis 5, where was the last time in the Bible that the word "death" or "die" appeared? Just two chapters earlier, in Genesis 3:

> "Now the serpent was more crafty than any of the wild animals the Lord God had made. He said to the woman, "Did God really say, 'you must not eat from any tree in the garden?'"
>
> The woman said to the serpent, "We may eat from the trees in the garden, but God did say, 'you must not eat from the tree that is in the middle of the garden, and you must not touch it, or you will die.'"
>
> "You will not surely die," the serpent said to the woman, "for God knows that when you eat of it, your eyes will be opened and you will be like God, knowing good and evil." (Gen 3:1-5)

The serpent lied. Adam's death in Genesis 5:5 is the first time the word death is used in the Bible since the conversation with the snake. People have died. Abel was killed. Lamech swore bloody vengeance. However, the last we heard of death was the serpent saying, "you will not surely die, for God knows that when you eat of it, you will become like God, knowing good and evil." The next time the word is used is at the death of Adam.

I think we are intended to make a connection between these two events, these two occurrences of the word "death." The serpent lied. Adam and Eve ate the fruit and death became reality for us. A second clause had to be added to the story of every human being that would follow:

Altogether, he lived *and then he died*. The serpent lied about the consequences of sin. He said "you will not surely die," but Adam and all his sons and daughters died. In the gospels, Jesus calls Satan the father of lies and we already see it here.

The simple repetition of the phrase "and then he died" calls us back to the very reason this sentence is pronounced. Adam and Eve believed the lies of the serpent, ate the fruit, broke relationship with God, fell under the curse, and entered into the consequences. The serpent lied. Sin has consequences that we feel to this day. You and I will die.

"After his own likeness"

Something else is said about Seth in these verses. Despite being different from Cain and having children who will call on the name of the Lord, he is still like his father, Adam.

> "This is the written account of Adam's line.
>
> When God created man, he made him in the likeness of God. He created them male and female and blessed them. And when they were created, he called them 'man.'
>
> When Adam had lived 130 years, he had a son in his own likeness, in his own image, and he named him Seth." (Genesis 5:1-3)

Adam had a son in his own likeness. "When God created man, he made him in the likeness of God" (5:1). But when Adam had a son, he had a son in *his own* likeness. His son was just like him. Adam was a sinner and he had a son in his own likeness.

The hardest part of having kids is that they are yours. Children carry the characteristics of their parents. Not just physical characteristics like height, eye color, or nose shape.

The Sinews of Scripture

We also carry temperaments and character from our parents. How often have we looked at a child and said sweetly, "Oh, she is just like her mother" and not five seconds later cringed and said, "Ooh, she is just like her mother." Parents look at their children and see their own likeness — their own faults, their own obsessions, their own bad habits. Sometimes, the hardest part of having kids is that they are just like you.

Adam had a son in his own likeness. A sinner. And Seth had Enosh and Enosh had Kenan and Kenan had Mahalalel and so on. The whole human race, men and women, are now not just in the likeness and image of God, but in the likeness and image of Adam and Eve.

If your grandparents were sinners, then so are your parents, and if your parents were sinners, then so are you, and if you are, then so are your kids. The truth revealed in Genesis 1 is that we are all made in the image of God, created and blessed, but the truth of Genesis 5 is that we are also each in the image and likeness of Adam.

The Promised Comforter

Genesis 5 ends with a promise. So far, there has been little encouragement in these genealogies. They have pointed to the reality of sin, its spread, and its consequences. They foreshadow the disastrous events of Babel. Yet, in spite of human sinfulness, God makes a promise:

> "When Lamech had lived 182 years, he had a son. He named him Noah, and said, "He will comfort us in our labor and the painful toil of our hands caused by the ground God has cursed."" (Genesis 5:28-29)

He will comfort us. He will give us relief from the curse

– the curse upon the ground and within our hearts. Lamech received a promise that there would be comfort and relief. It was a shadow of a promise that the curse would not last forever, that sin would not ultimately claim victory, and that this reversing of the curse would begin with Noah.

"He will comfort us in our labor and the painful toil of our hands caused by the ground the Lord has cursed."

Our comfort in the midst of the curse would begin with Noah. Noah will be faithful, will build an ark, and will be rescued when the flood of destruction and cleansing comes. God will make a new beginning with Noah. However, our promised comfort is about more than Noah. The promise did not truly find its fulfillment in Noah, but in another — Jesus Christ. Our comfort comes from one born in Adam's line, like us in every way except for sin (Hebrews 4:15). The comfort comes from one who was not made simply *in* the image of God, but *is* the very image of God himself. Jesus Christ who lived — *and then he died*. The verdict we hear pronounced over and over again upon the sons of Adam in Genesis 5 is something the second Adam, Jesus Christ, takes upon himself. He lived and then he died.

"And then he died" is not the end of Jesus' life. Jesus Christ rose from the dead to bring comfort and relief. He fulfilled what was spoken over Noah: "He will comfort us in our labor and the painful toil of our hands caused by the ground the Lord has cursed." Jesus gives not only rest from the work of our hands, but deliverance from the work of our hands. He brings not only forgiveness, but a reversal of the destiny of those caught in the consequences of sin.

Genesis 5 presents a world where the human race is born in the likeness of Adam and the phrase "and then he died" seems like the last word on human life. Yet, Lamech received a promise. He didn't live to see it fulfilled, but in

Jesus, "and then he died" is not the end. In Jesus, there is life, then death, and then life again.

As Paul put it, "For if, by the trespass of the one man, death reigned through that one man, how much more will those who receive God's abundant provision of grace and of the gift of righteousness reign in life through the one man, Jesus Christ!" (Romans 5:17)

The promise of relief given to Lamech was fulfilled in Christ. Jesus provides relief from living in the way of Adam so that we can live in the image of God. Jesus also reverses the last line of every person in this genealogy by providing life after death. In Jesus Christ, the promise of Noah is kept.

Conclusion

The first two genealogies in the Bible already serve as sinews connecting the whole Biblical story together. In the genealogies of Cain and Seth, we have a mirror held up to see our own condition as sons and daughters of Adam. We see the consequences of the lie the serpent told (and our first parents believed). Sin has burrowed its way into the human condition and given birth to death. Already Genesis 5 recalls us back to Genesis 3, where the the first Adam trusted the serpent, and propels us ahead to the second Adam, who crushed the head of the serpent in his life, death, and resurrection.

Discussion Questions:

1. How is the genealogy of Cain different than the genealogy of Seth? What do those differences tell us?

2. Genesis 5 says that Adam had a son "in his own likeness." Describe a time you have seen a child look or act in the same way as a parent.

3. How does the repeated phrase "and then he died" in Genesis 5 point to Jesus?

4. Is the end or the beginning of Genesis 5 more important? Why do you think that?

Expansion & Narrowing Genealogies:

Genesis 10-11

"These are the descendants of Shem, by their families, their languages, their lands, and their nations." – Genesis 10:31

Repetition in the Bible is a clue to pay attention. When the Bible was first written, the process of writing, copying, binding, and even producing paper or papyrus was expensive and time consuming. There are no wasted words in the Bible. This is not only because the Holy Spirit was guiding the composition and preservation of these texts, but because wasted words were costly. So when the Bible repeats something, we should sit up and take notice. In Genesis 10 and 11, a significant portion of the descendants of Shem are listed twice. Genesis 10:21-31 lists the family of Shem, including the likes of Arphaxad, Shelah, Eber, and Peleg. However, after the tower of Babel, we get another genealogy of Shem (Gen. 11:10-32), including repeating the same people for the first five generations.

The line of Shem is repeated twice because each instance of his genealogy serves a different purpose. In this chapter, we will look at the two dominant patterns of genealogies in the Bible as they appear in the two genealogies of Genesis 10 and 11. In addition, we will explore the interlude at the tower of Babel and how it fits within these two family lists. The goal is to give us some broader tools with which to understand how to read any genealogy we encounter in the Bible.

Two Directions of a Genealogy: Expansion and Narrowing

Broadly speaking, there are two different kinds of genealogies in the Bible: expansion and narrowing. Some genealogies expand from one person into many descendants. This is the most common way we structure our own family genealogies. There is one ancestral couple — whether four or fourteen generations ago — and the genealogy lists their children, their children's children, and those children's children's children all the way down. From two people comes a huge family, a web of people connected to a common ancestor. We see these "expansion genealogies" in Numbers and Ezra. Each tribe is listed, then the sons and their families, then the families that came from them. As an Israelite hearing those lists, it might have been exciting to wait to hear the name of your family. Expansion genealogies emphasize connection. All these various people are actually deeply connected to one another. Throughout later chapters we will cover several expansion genealogies: the descendants of Esau, Ishmael, and Israel. Their purpose is to show the connection between these various people as they spread across the globe.

Expansion genealogies also show the fulfillment of God's commands in Genesis 1. "God blessed them, and God said to them, "Be fruitful and multiply, and fill the earth and subdue it; and have dominion over the fish of the sea and over the birds of the air and over every living thing that moves upon the earth.""(Gen. 1:28). This command — sometimes known as the "Creation Mandate" — involves the growth and spread of humanity across the world. The command was repeated after the devastation of the flood (Gen. 9:7). These expansion genealogies show the earth being filled with people. When it comes to the specific genealogies of Israel, expansion genealogies also connect with God's promise to Abraham to give him children "like the dust of the earth; so that if one can count the dust of the earth, [his] offspring also can be counted" (Gen. 13:16). Whether as genealogies of God's people or the nations, expansion genealogies emphasize the connection between various peoples and God's promise to fill the earth.

However, other genealogies begin with huge families and nations and narrow down to one person. In narrowing genealogies, the person at the end of the genealogy is more important than the person at the beginning. The power of the genealogy is at its conclusion, not its beginning. Not every single ancestor is included, but the genealogy traces one single family line down to an important individual within God's purpose of salvation. We saw this already in Genesis 5, where the genealogy of Seth names that people "had many other sons and daughters," but only follows the one son until it reaches Noah. We will see this again in the genealogy of Abraham, Isaac, and Jacob. There are multiple children, but the promise remains with one. So the genealogy narrows and even excludes. Only with the sons of Jacob will the genealogy expand again, when the covenant extends not just to one man, but to an entire people. However, even then, the promise of kingship rests with just one tribe — Judah. At the end of Ruth, the genealogy narrows to the birth of David. However, the most prominent example of a narrowing genealogy is found in the opening verses of the Gospel of Matthew. There, the children of Abraham are followed all the way down to one man: Jesus Christ. The power of the genealogy is found in its conclusion, not in its beginning.

Narrowing genealogies emphasize the fulfillment of God's promises. In particular, they show how God keeps his covenantal promises, the gospel promises. All the way back in Genesis 3:15, we hear God tell the serpent,

"And I will put enmity
between you and the woman,
and between your offspring and hers;
he will crush your head,
and you will strike his heel."

One of the great purposes of biblical genealogies is the search for this promised offspring of Eve who would crush the head of the serpent. Every narrowing genealogy shows the promise carrying forward. The narrow genealogies of Abraham and David show how the promise, not just the promise made to Eve, but the covenant made with Abraham and David, continues in a narrow way with a particular line. This narrowing continues all the way down to the person of Jesus, who is the fulfillment of all the great promises of God.

The expansion genealogies begin with one great ancestor and trace the many families and generations that flow from him. These genealogies emphasize the connection between various peoples and God's promise to fill the earth. The narrowing genealogies end with the fulfillment of God's promise. They exclude many people and many details to bring us down to the one that God has chosen to carry forward the covenantal plan of salvation.

Genesis 10 and 11 contain two overlapping genealogies: one expansion and one narrowing. By looking at both (and the brief, but significant, interlude at the tower of Babel), we will see more clearly how to read expansion and narrowing genealogies more generally.

Expansion: The Descendants of Noah

Genesis 10 lists the descendants of Noah after the flood. At the conclusion we are told that "These are the families of Noah's sons, according to their genealogies, in their nations; and from these the nations spread abroad on the earth after the flood" (10:32). Sometimes known as "the Table of the Nations," this expansion genealogy shows the various descendants of Noah spreading across the globe and filling the earth (in accordance with God's command in Genesis 9:7). The genealogy is divided into three parts, corresponding with each of Noah's three sons: Shem, Ham, and Japheth. Each section follows a similar pattern: the first generation of sons are listed, then one or more of those children have their children listed, before ending with a description of their territory. For example, the genealogy of Ham ends with "And the territory of the Canaanites extended from Sidon, in the direction of Gera, as far as Gaza, and in the direction of Sodom, Gomorrah, Admah, and Zeboiim, as far as Lasha. These are the descendants of Ham, by their families, their languages, their lands, and their nations" (10:19-20).

As an expansion genealogy, the genealogy of Noah serves two purposes. First, it connects various peoples together. There is one human race, even if there are many nations spread across the globe. Through the years, people have noted that many of these names correspond to nations in the world.

Japheth's family settled along the coastlands (10:5), likely referring to the Mediterranean Sea. Some of Japheth's sons have Hebrew names that might have more familiar equivalents in Greek. Madai might refer to the Medes, Javan to the Ionians, and Ashkenaz to the Scythians. Tarshish was a far-off land to the west, possibly near the strait of Gibraltar. Kittim might refer to Kition on Cyprus and Rodanim to the island of Rhodes. We cannot know for sure, but many have seen the sons of Japheth as the ancestors of the Greeks.

Ham's family settled in North Africa and Arabia. Cush is another name for Ethiopia. Egypt is a nation in north Africa and Put is modern day Libya. Sheba and Havilah were both nations mentioned elsewhere in the Bible and renowned for their wealth. Canaan was both the name of the land that later encompassed Israel and the surrounding area, but the person, Canaan, became the ancestor of many of the peoples that would plague Israel's time in the land: Jebusites, Amorites, Girgashites, Hivites, Arkites, and more. Nimrod was the founder of Babel and Assyria and gave birth to the Philistines, many of the great enemies of Israel.

The descendants of Shem settled in western Asia. Elam, Asshur (Assyria), Arpachshad (Chaldea), Lud (Lydia), and Aram are all nations. Like all genealogies, the family of Noah is intended to connect backward and forward in the Biblical story. Many of the nations that Israel encounters and struggles against throughout history find their origin here. However, its greater purpose is to help us see that all these nations are connected together. All of these people come from the family of Noah. They are all the fruits of those who survived the devastation of the flood.

The second purpose is to show the fulfillment of the command "be fruitful and multiple, abound on the earth and multiply in it" (9:7). Though the list of names does not cover every conceivable place on the planet, it encompasses the breadth of the known world at that time. The descendants of Noah spread to every corner of the globe. At the end of each section of the genealogy it lists the territories of these families, claiming they have broad lands, languages, and nations.

Wait a minute. The descendants of Ham, Shem, and Japheth had different languages and spread across the earth in Genesis chapter 10? How can that be when everyone had the same language and was gathered in the same place at the beginning of chapter 11?

Genealogies record generations, but they do not always serve as the sole bridge across a gap in time. In Genesis 4 and 5, the only record we have between Adam and Noah is the genealogy. It serves as the only bridge between those two periods. However, with the genealogy of David at the end of Ruth, we have one bridge, but certainly not the only one. Judges and 1 Samuel also cover the same period overlapping with the lives of Ruth and Boaz and reaching all the way to David. So Ruth can end with the genealogy of David, while 1 Samuel begins before the birth of David. Ishmael and Esau's genealogies also march ahead of the story in which they are placed. The genealogies themselves stretch generations into the future, but once the genealogy is done, the story picks up right where it left off. Something similar is happening between Genesis 10 and 11. The genealogy includes information both before and after the tower of Babel. The expansion genealogy in Genesis 10 propels us forward toward when the world is filled and the people do spread across the face of the earth with their own languages, but then Genesis 11 pauses and interjects a story that took place prior to that full spread.

Interlude: The Tower of Babel

Babel is a story of disobedience. God commanded them to spread and fill the earth, but when the people after the flood reached the plains of Shinar, they stopped and settled. They intentionally did not want to be spread across the earth, so they built "a tower with its top in the heavens" (11:4). They intentionally and willfully disobeyed God. However, God's will would not be thwarted. Though they built a tall tower, the God who is seated on the throne of heaven "came down to see the city and the tower" (11:5). God saw what they were doing and confused their languages. "So the LORD scattered them abroad from there over the face of all the earth, and they left off building the city" (11:8).

Babel is also a story of pride. It was not simply that they did not want to obey the Lord, but they wanted to "make a name for themselves" (11:4). The goal of the tower was to elevate *their* name – their status, their legacy, their glory and honor. The devastating judgment of the flood upon the human race, whose every inclination of the thoughts of their hearts was only evil continually (6:5), did little to humble humanity. God had wiped away every living thing but what was contained in the ark, but still they sought to make a name for themselves, to exalt and elevate themselves. God came down and saw the city and the tower and said, "this is only the beginning of what they will do" (11:6) and humbled the proud by confusing and scattering them. The interlude of the story of Babel is both an example of pride being humbled and God's plan for creation moving forward despite human disobedience.

However, the story of Babel also serves as a good hinge between the expansion genealogy of Noah and the narrowing genealogy of Shem. God's purpose is not the consolidation and uniformity of creation. God's work is expansive and diverse. He creates not just one, but thousands of different kinds of beautiful flowers. He creates not just one, but hundreds of thousands of kinds of birds and fish and animals that move along the ground. There is both a unity and diversity to God's creation. The human race is held together, it is one, yet it is also multi-faceted. The spread is part of God's intention and design, but the confusion that comes with it is part of the consequence of sin.

Yet in the midst of this good unity and diversity, God does call specific people to participate in his work of salvation. Babel was a prideful attempt of humanity to narrow the scope of God's plan in the world. Humanity sought to narrow, to gather, and to make a name for themselves. This is a stark contrast with the sons of Eber that make up the genealogy of Genesis 11. They did not make their name great, but by letting God narrow his plan to one family, God made a great name for them.

Narrowing: The Descendants of Shem

By the time we get to the genealogy of Genesis 11, we have travelled through the scattering of Babel. As we read this second genealogy, we will notice that some of the names and information is a repetition of what we heard already in the previous chapter. The same names appear in both genealogies: Shem, Arpachshad, Shelah, Eber, and Peleg. However, now these names have a different purpose. Instead of showing the expansion of the human race across the whole earth, the genealogy of Shem in Genesis 11 shows God's promise to redeem, his promise to send a child who will crush the head of the serpent, is being continued through one man, Abram, child of Eber, child of Shem.

Instead of continuing through powerful nations like Egypt, Babylon, or Assyria, our story will continue through the small line of Eber, from whom we get the name Hebrew. Genesis 10 zooms out to give us a glimpse of this full creation that God loves and is redeeming. But Genesis 11 narrows down to the one family through whom God would bring about this redemption. The power of Genesis 11 is not at the beginning of the genealogy, but at the end.

Yet, in his grand, gracious plan to redeem the whole creation, including the powerful nations whose ancestors are named in Genesis 10 — God chooses to work through ordinary people of faith.

After the nations spread out across the earth and the population soars, God chooses one man, Abram, through whom he will bless the whole earth. The genealogy of Shem is a narrowing genealogy, which means its power comes at the end. Shem and Eber's line continues all the way to a man named Abram and his wife, Sarai.

God's plan to restore relationship with the human race includes his gracious work through ordinary people of faith. The story of the rest of the Bible does not take place in the grand halls of power, but first in one man, then one family, then one nation, into whom the Son of God would take on flesh, live, breathe, die, and rise again so that this life, this abundant and free life, this gracious relationship with Father, Son, and Holy Spirit might spread to the far corners of the globe.

Genesis 10 lists often powerful names, but more often than not, God chooses to use ordinary people by the gracious work of the Holy Spirit to form faith in others.

Conclusion

There are two basic patterns of genealogies in the Bible. Some begin with a single person or couple and list the generations that follow, expanding into an entire people or nation. We see this expansion genealogy in the genealogy of Noah in Genesis 10. This pattern emphasizes connection between people and God's work of fulfilling his promise to fill the land or the world with people. The most important figure in the genealogy is at the beginning. Other genealogies are more selective. They narrow the focus to name only specific children who will carry on the promise of God. The goal of this pattern is carrying forward the covenant promise that there would be a child of Eve who would crush the head of the serpent. The most important figure in these genealogies is always at the end. We see this narrowing genealogy in the genealogy of Shem in Genesis 11. While Genesis 10 shows Shem's line expanding to fill regions of the earth, Genesis 11 shows it narrowing down to one man, Abram, and his wife, Sarai, who will soon receive the covenantal promise of God.

Being able to identify whether a genealogy is expanding or narrowing is a skill that will aid us in reading all the other genealogies of the Bible. The same set of family names can serve a very different purpose when presented differently. Expanding genealogies emphasize connection while narrowing genealogies emphasize fulfillment of the promise. We will see this again vividly in the two genealogies of Jesus in Matthew and Luke.

Discussion Questions:

1. What are the two different types of genealogies? What do each of them communicate?

2. How does the genealogy in Genesis 10 show the connection between people after the flood? Why would that be important for us to know?

3. How does the Tower of Babel fit into the story of Genesis 10 and 11?

4. Who is the most important person in the genealogy of Shem? How does this genealogy connect to the bigger story of God's redemption?

The Pattern of Patience:

Genesis 25

"Isaac loved Esau, because he was fond of game; but Rebekah loved Jacob." – Genesis 25:28

Many of us struggle to know what to do when we come across a family tree with a list of sons we have never met. We read them, but they wash over us like the numbers on the stock ticker on the bottom of the television screen. They are words that seem to have no meaning. However, if all Scripture is God-breathed and useful — if there are no throwaway lines in the Bible — then all three genealogies in Genesis 25 have something to say to us.

There is a consistent pattern in Genesis 25 that continues throughout the biblical genealogies: patience. God's people must learn to wait upon God's promises. In this chapter, we will first get a handle on the "pattern of patience" by focusing on Abraham's children with Keturah and the sons of Ishmael. Then, we will look at the role patience plays both in Isaac and Rebekah and in Jacob and Esau.

THE PATTERN OF PATIENCE: GENESIS 25:1-18

There is a pattern of patience in the genealogies in the Bible. God's people seem to have to wait longer for blessing than those who are not a part of God's people. God calls Abram and promises to bless him, promises that all nations will be blessed through him (Gen. 12:1-3). God promises to give him descendants as numerous as the sand on the seashore and the stars in the sky (Gen. 22:17). This is the promise — a great nation, multitudes of descendants, and eventually through the seed of Abraham, the blessing of the whole world. Abraham has God's promise, but Abraham's brother Nahor has twelve sons. Abraham struggles until he is eighty-six to have one son and that son is through Sarah's slave-girl, Hagar. God even says that Ishmael is not the child of promise, not the one through whom God will fulfill his promise to Abraham. So Abraham and Sarah struggle until he is one hundred years old before Isaac is born.

Step back a second. Abraham is promised the abundant blessing of children. Nahor, who has not been given this promise, has twelve children. Abraham, after one hundred years, has two sons. Well, actually only one, since Isaac alone carries the promise of God. It all seems to come more easily to Nahor than Abraham. Abraham has to wait longer. After Isaac, the promised child, is married to Rebekah and the responsibility of carrying forward God's covenant promise is handed over to Isaac, Abraham marries Keturah. Now Abraham has six more sons – Zimran, Jokshan, Medan, Midian, Ishbak, and Shuah. These sons have sons who, in turn, have more sons. Yet, these are not sons of the promise, these are not the children God promised when he called Abraham out of Ur. They only come after the covenant has been passed on to Isaac. Everything seems harder for those who carry the promise than those who do not.

We go to the next generation and see Ishmael, who is the not the promised child, has twelve children, who become twelve princes. Isaac and Rebekah spend twenty years barren and then have two sons. Of Jacob and Esau, only Jacob will carry on the covenant. It is only when Jacob himself has twelve sons – all of whom will be part of the people, the twelve tribes of Israel – do we finally begin to see the fulfillment of the promise. Nahor has twelve children on the first generation, Abraham has to wait three generations. Ishmael has twelve children on the first generation, Isaac has to wait two generations.

This is the pattern of patience. God's people have to wait longer to see with their eyes and touch with their hands the blessings God has promised. Nahor has twelve sons. Ishmael has twelve sons. Faithful Abraham has two, but only one bears the promises. Isaac has two, but only one bears the promise. Over and over again, the people of God must be patient, waiting for God's promised future. Nahor and Ishmael have their full material blessing in the present, but for Abraham, for Isaac, for the people of God, the fullness of God's blessing lies in the future.

This pattern of patience runs contrary to the so-called prosperity gospel that has so much influence in the North American church. Prosperity gospel teachers claim that we can have our best life now, that if we simply trust God's promise of blessing, if we name the promise and claim it for our own, then God will rain down material blessings in our lives.

This is not what we actually see in the Bible. The life of Abraham and Isaac puts the lie to this claim. Abraham believed the Lord and it was credited to him as righteousness (Gen. 15:6), but he never lived to see the twelve tribes of Israel. He died when Jacob and Esau were fifteen. If anyone could have named the promise and claimed it, it was Abraham. If anyone could be said to have enough faith, it was Abraham, and yet he had to wait.

So we have a contrast. With Nahor and Ishmael, everything is right now. There is immediate blessing and immediate gratification. There is no need to look for the future, no need to look for anything else. But with Abraham and Isaac, they must learn to wait. They wait generations to see God keeps his promises, but this builds in them a deeper trust in the Lord and directs their gaze toward the future. God trains his people to trust his promise over what seems immediately gratifying in the present.

Isaac and Rebekah: Genesis 25:19-28

This pattern of patience plays out in the lives of Isaac and Rebekah, as well as Jacob and Esau. There is a stark difference between those who impatiently want blessing now and those who learn to wait upon the Lord. After twenty years of waiting and praying, Rebekah is finally pregnant, but there is a war in her womb. She seeks a Word from the LORD and hears,

"Two nations are in your womb,
and two peoples born of you shall be divided;
the one shall be stronger than the other,
the elder shall serve the younger." (Gen 25:23)

Rebekah is told, before the children are born, that the younger of the two is to be the leader, is the one chosen by God.

Outwardly, Esau looks the part. He was red and hairy – a symbol of glory. He was a hunter. On the outside, he is the perfect candidate to carry on the promise, to take over the kingdom from Isaac. However, Rebekah knows, based upon the Word from the LORD, that Esau is not to be the heir. She knows that despite his outward appearance, it is the second son, Jacob, who will be the heir to the kingdom and the promise.

When Jacob comes out of the womb, we have no description of what he looks like. All we know is that he is grasping the heel of his brother Esau. He follows literally on his brother's heels, but has no distinguishing features. But Rebekah knows that he is the one. She has received the promise of God, his Word that the older son will serve the younger, and she trusts the promise.

While all outward appearances point to Esau as the glorious son, God has chosen Jacob. God has chosen the younger, the lesser, the weak things of this world in order to shame the strong (1 Cor 1:27). So, trusting in the Word of the Lord, Jacob should be recognized as heir to the kingdom and heir to the promises of God.

But what happens? "Isaac loved Esau, because he was fond of game, but Rebekah loved Jacob" (Gen. 25:28).

What is wrong with this picture? For starters, there is division in the family. Mom and Dad favor different children. But it goes deeper. Isaac loved Esau because he was fond of game. Esau was a hunter and he brought home meat for Isaac to eat. Esau was Isaac's favorite son because he filled his belly. Isaac sinned by considering what he saw on the outside and what was personally satisfying to him, instead of trusting in what God had said to be true. However, Rebekah loved Jacob because she trusted the Word of God. Jacob is the one chosen by God, not Esau. So what is troubling about Isaac and Rebekah is not just the damaged family dynamics, but that one parent is trusting in the Word of God, trusting in the promise of God revealed in his Word, and the other is trusting what fills his stomach, trusting his judgment over God's, his desires over what God has declared to be true.

Among other things, Isaac demonstrates an impatience when he favors Esau. Esau is able to fill his belly right now. The satisfaction he gets from having Esau as a son is immediate. The blessings that come from Esau come right now, today, in my mouth and in my stomach. Instead of the patience that looks to God's promise, Isaac wants immediate fulfillment and blessing. It is a trait he will pass on to Esau himself.

"Isaac loved Esau, because he was fond of game, but Rebekah loved Jacob." (25:28) The sin of Isaac in favoring Esau creates all sorts of trouble in the story moving forward. But Rebekah will trust God's Word, and work to bring it to fulfillment.

JACOB AND ESAU

The difference between patiently waiting for the blessing and wanting immediate fulfillment will follow this family into the next generation. From the very beginning the two brothers are set over against one another as polar opposites. "When the boys grew up, Esau was a skillful hunter, a man of the field, while Jacob was a quiet man, living in tents." (Gen. 25:27)

Esau was a hunter, Jacob was a quiet man - literally a "perfect, complete, sound, or wholesome man." Esau was a man of the field, Jacob lived in tents. When Esau was hungry, he went out into the wild, killed an animal, brought it home and ate it. Whenever he got hungry again, he would go out, kill and eat. Rinse and repeat. Esau is not a man of forethought, a man of planning. Jacob, by contrast, lives in tents. That does not mean he was an "indoorsman," but that he stayed on the farm with the livestock. Jacob would work with the animals during the day, manage the books, and then come back and sleep in the tent at night. He was a shepherd. Jacob was being prepared for the responsibility of leading the kingdom. We learn later, in his time with his uncle, Laban, that Jacob was very good with breeding animals and managing the herd. Esau would go out into the land to hunt and often would not sleep in the tents, sleeping on the ground.

The difference between the two is seen already in the first story we have of the brothers. Esau comes in from hunting and obviously has not caught anything, since he is famished. He is not starving to death, but simply hungry. He sees Jacob making a stew and wants some of it. At this point, Esau does not even know what Jacob is making. He just calls it "red stuff" (Gen. 25:30). For a man like Esau, when he is hungry it is the only thing on his mind. He gets tunnel vision. It does not even matter what Jacob is cooking. He wants it.

Jacob holds off, asking him to sell him his birthright. According to God's Word to Rebekah, the birthright should already have been Jacob's. He was to be the heir. However, because Isaac sinned by favoring Esau, Jacob had to find another way to get what should have been his. We should not be too hard on Jacob here. Remember that Esau is not starving. Esau claims he is about to die, but the Bible only says that he is famished (25:29). He is not on death's door.

"Jacob said, "First sell me your birthright." Esau said, "I am about to die, of what use is a birthright to me." (25:32). Esau basically says, "what does the future matter when I am hungry right now?" What use is my inheritance when that red stuff looks so good right now? What use is all that has been given to me, all that my father will pass to me, when I am hungry right now? What use are the promises of God, when I want *it* — give me some of that red stuff.

Esau is a man who only thinks of the present. He will inherit in the distant future, whenever Isaac dies. Esau is not patient and has no concern for that time, only for right now. This is part of being a hunter. He is not a farmer. He lives moment by moment. When he is hungry, he goes to hunt for more food. Part of maturity is learning to have a longer sense of time. Children do not have this naturally. They think only of the present and of their immediate needs. They must be taught to look farther than this moment. Jacob has a different sense of time than Esau. Jacob will need to continue to develop this. He must work seven years for a wife and seven for another. This is a different sense of time than we usually have. We have a very immediate culture – focused on the present and very little sense of the past or future.

Thus Esau despised his birthright. He considered it worthless. He sold it for a pot of stew. He took what would have nourished him for a lifetime and threw it away for what would fill his belly in the moment. He took what was a supreme gift and threw it away to satisfy his immediate hungers. He gave up the future for a quick fix in the present.

"Esau was given bread and lentil stew, he ate and drank, rose and went his way. Thus he despised his birthright." (Gen. 25:34)

Jacob sought the birthright. He valued his place in the covenant. Was he greedy for a larger inheritance and hoping to get a victory over his brother? Perhaps, but the Bible does not say that. However, we do see that Jacob was patient. A birthright is much more valuable than a pot of stew. But only if you look beyond the moment, beyond the immediate desire for food. A birthright could take many years before you receive your inheritance. In fact, Jacob would soon flee from Esau's rage and live apart from his family for decades before he would return and the two sons would bury their father (Gen 35:29). The promised inheritance won here for a pot of stew would take decades to come to fulfillment. But what Jacob received – in the covenantal blessing of God – would be far greater than what he traded to Esau.

There is a pattern of patience in the genealogies and stories of God's people. Rebekah waited twenty years barren, hoping for children. Both barrenness and the blessing of children are so often intertwined in the story of God's people, in God's working out of his plan of redemption. God promised Rebekah that, of her two children, it was the younger Jacob, not the older, more impressive looking Esau who would be the heir of the promise of redemption. There is also a pattern of impatience that interrupts the people's trust in God. Isaac sinned by ignoring God's Word and considering only what he could see on the outside, what satisfied his stomach in the moment. Esau also despised the promise of God, the blessed future, in favor of a pot of stew that would fill him only for a moment.

Conclusion

What enabled the people of God to forgo what might seem easy and satisfying in the moment in favor of something they could not see? What let Abraham and Isaac not give up when the blessings seemed to come easier and faster to others than for them? What enabled Rebekah to trust in God's Word about her children, even if she could not yet see evidence of it with her eyes? What caused Jacob to seek diligently the birthright, while Esau despised it?

In other words, what lets God's people have their feet in the present with their eyes to the future?

They held fast to God's promise. At the center of the biblical story is the drama of the birth of a child. Going all the way back to the garden, there was the promise that God would send a child of Eve who would crush the head of the serpent, undoing and setting right all that had been so grievously set wrong by sin. Generation after generation, the people awaited the birth of that child. God promised that it would come from the seed of Abraham, then narrowed it through Isaac, then Jacob, then Judah, then the house of David. Throughout the way, God opened barren wombs and protected threatened children. There was always the temptation to let go of the promise, to let go of trusting in the LORD in favor of what seemed to give immediate results, to give immediate relief. Every generation of God's people faced the temptation to love Esau because he fills our bellies or to sell the birthright for a pot of stew. Yet, even when they did, God continued to work out his redemption. Every generation got closer to the promise, but they did not know when it would come. They held on to the promise that God would one day send the child. Then an angel appeared to a virgin named Mary, telling her she would have a son who would finally be the promised child. The covenant carried by Abraham and Sarah, Isaac and Rebekah, and Jacob passed down to the people of Israel finally found its true purpose at the coming of Jesus Christ. As the writer of Hebrews said,

> "All these people were still living by faith when they died. They did not receive the things promised; they only saw them and welcomed them from a distance, admitting that they were

foreigners and strangers on earth. People who say such things show that they are looking for a country of their own. If they had been thinking of the country they had left, they would have had opportunity to return. Instead, they were longing for a better country—a heavenly one. Therefore God is not ashamed to be called their God, for he has prepared a city for them."
(Hebrews 11:13-16)

Though these promises have been fulfilled in Jesus Christ, Christians continue to wait for all God's promises to come true. Yet, we live in a world that does not prize patience. We are pushed to want results or success quickly and visibly. Yet, like Abraham, we must often learn to wait patiently while those around us more easily and quickly experience the material blessings of the world. We will only learn to live patiently when, like Abraham, our hearts are set on a better country — the city of God.

Discussion Questions

1. Describe a time where you have had to wait patiently for God. What strengthened you during that time?

2. How would you describe the difference between Isaac and Rebekah in this story? Between Jacob and Esau? How did these differences impact what happened in the story?

3. There is always a temptation for us to want immediate fulfillment in our faith, like Esau. How can we grow more patient like Jacob in our faith?

The Ghosts of Esau:

Genesis 36

"I have endeavoured in this Ghostly little book, to raise the Ghost of an Idea, which shall not put my readers out of humour with themselves, with each other, with the season, or with me. May it haunt their houses pleasantly, and no one wish to lay it."
– Charles Dickens

Ebenezer Scrooge was not a kind man. He begins Charles Dickens' *A Christmas Carol* as a cold-hearted miser. Despite his misery and the misery he causes others, Scrooge is unaware of himself until visited during the night by three ghosts: The Ghost of Christmas Past, the Ghost of Christmas Present, and the Ghost of Christmas Yet to Come. These ghosts reveal to Scrooge who he has been and the consequences for others of the path that he has walked. This triple encounter changes Scrooge. In Dickens' phrase, it "haunts him pleasantly." Seeing the past, present, and future confronted Scrooge with himself and led to a change in heart and life.

The genealogy of Esau is a bit like *A Christmas Carol*. In

it, Israel — and thus, the church — is confronted with her past, present, and future. She is shown the path of Esau and the bitter fruit it bears. Yet, the hope for us all is that time spent in Esau's genealogy would "haunt us pleasantly." It should linger in our souls, but in a way that leads us away from the path of Esau and deeper along the path of faithfulness to God.

In examining the genealogy of Esau, we will explore how it connects with past, present, or future people and events in the Bible.

THE GHOST OF ESAU PAST: LOT

> "Then Esau took his wives, his sons, his daughters, and all the members of his household, his cattle, all his livestock, and all the property he had acquired in the land of Canaan; and he moved to a land some distance from his brother Jacob. For their possessions were too great for them to live together; the land where they were staying could not support them because of their livestock. So Esau settled in the hill country of Seir; Esau is Edom." (Genesis 36:6-8)

After Esau has sons in Canaan, he takes all he has and separates from Jacob. He separates because the land where they were staying could not support them. Where have we heard that before? Where else does a relative separate from the chosen covenant people of God because the land itself could not support their large flocks and livestock? Lot and Abraham.

When Abraham and his nephew Lot enter the land of Canaan, they both have large flocks and herds. Abram is described as "very rich in livestock" (Gen. 13:2) and Lot also had flocks and herds so that "the land could not support both of them living together; for their possessions were so great that they could not live together" (13:6). In order to keep from quarreling over food and water, the two men agreed to separate and settle in different places. Abram gives Lot the first choice of land. Lot chooses the well-watered plain of Jordan, which looked like the garden of Eden, like Egypt (Gen 13:10). This is the land of Sodom and Gomorrah. Lot settles there, but within a couple chapters, we find that the outcry against the wickedness of those cities is so great that the Lord will destroy them. Through the intercession of Abraham and the work of two angels, Lot is saved, but at great cost. The cities are destroyed in God's judgment and Lot's wife is turned to a pillar of salt.

Lot's separation from Abram initially looks like a blessing, but ends in destruction. He picks the best looking land and he prospers there. However, he chooses prosperity over being near to the promise of God (something we already saw from Esau in Genesis 25). This separation ends in disaster.

Esau separates from Jacob for the same reason Lot separated from Abram. This repetition of phrases and reasons tells us that we are supposed to see Esau as a Lot-like character. When Lot separates from the people of God, he settles near Sodom and the story turns toward judgment and destruction. As we will see shortly, it may look different, but the same thing happens to Esau when he separates from Jacob. Genesis 36 invites us to see Lot and Esau side-by-side in order to see how their stories line up with each other. This connection backwards helps us understand that Esau separating from Jacob is a move toward judgment and destruction.

The Ghost of Esau Present: The People of the Land

"Esau took his wives from the Canaanites: Adah daughter of Elon the Hittite, Oholibamah daughter of Anah son of Zibeon the Hivite, and Basemath, Ishmael's daughter, sister of Nebaioth" (Genesis 36:2-3)

Esau's genealogy was a reminder to the people of Jacob (Israel) not to lose their identity as God's people. Esau is the twin of Jacob. Where Esau goes there is always the temptation that Jacob will follow. As the people of God, we face the temptation to walk the path of Esau. The path of Esau as we see in Genesis 36, is the story of a loss of identity.

The children of Abraham were to be a people set apart. Esau is a son of Isaac, and a descendant of Abraham. Abraham was called out of the nations to receive the promise of God. He was called to walk before God and be blameless (Gen. 17:1) and was promised that God would be his God and that God would bless all nations through the children of Abraham (Gen 12:1-3). As God would later tell Israel, "Now if you obey me fully and keep my covenant, then out of all nations you will be my treasured possession. Although the whole earth is mine, you will be for me a kingdom of priests and a holy nation" (Exodus 19:5-6). Abraham's descendants were called by God to bear witness to the Lord, his will, and his way in the world. Abraham's son, Isaac, carried these promises. He lived among the peoples of the land in Gerar, but maintained his distinctive identity as a child of Abraham, one called by God to bear the promise and the covenant. Isaac has two sons, twins, Jacob and Esau. By the end of Genesis 36, Esau and his people lose their distinctive identity and calling, and become so indistinguishable from the people of the land that we cannot tell where one ends and the other begins.

The people of Esau — the Edomites — and the inhabitants of the land — the Horites — become so intermarried and so intertwined that you cannot tell them apart. Lot separated from Abram and his life was almost destroyed. Esau leaves Jacob and his identity and distinctiveness is, in fact, destroyed.

Genesis 36 starts with the genealogy of Esau. It includes names like Oholibamah and Timna (36:2, 12). But when we get to verse 20, we see the genealogies of the inhabitants of the land and these names all show up again. Oholibamah is the daughter of Anah, son of Zibeon (36:25). Timna, who was the concubine that bore Amalek to Eliphaz, was the sister of Lotan (36:22). The people of Esau and the people of the land criss-cross so that once we get to the period of the kings of Edom, they are no longer considered two separate peoples. The children of Esau and the inhabitants of the land have become one, so that the children of Esau have lost their identity as children of Abraham.

Esau has three wives, all of whom come not from the people of God, but from the people of the land. Genesis 26 already hints that these marriages spell trouble, as "they made life bitter for Isaac and Rebekah" (26:35). Abraham sends a servant all the way back to Haran with the charge to "not get a wife for my son from the daughters of the Canaanites, among whom I live, but [go] to my country and my kindred and get a wife for my son, Isaac" (24:2-3). Abraham is so concerned about Isaac intermarrying with the people of the land that his servant travels hundreds of miles to find a wife for him. After Rebekah laments how miserable life is with Esau's foreign wives, Isaac sends Jacob hundreds of miles back to Haran to find a wife from their own people. But Esau marries women of the land. Adah is a Hittite. Oholibamah is a Hivite, and Basemath is an Ishmaelite.

The inter-marriage of Esau with the people of the land was not about race, but about religion and identity. Esau's genealogy is placed here as a warning to God's people not to lose their distinctive identity and calling in the world, not to become so merged with everyone else that they lose who they are and who God has called them to be.

This is the temptation faced continually by the people of God. We are called to be *in* the land, to be *in* the world, to be *in* every nation, yet we are called to be distinct. We have a different identity, a different calling. We belong to the LORD.

> "You are the salt of the earth, but if salt has lost its taste, how can its saltiness be restored? It is no longer good for anything, but is thrown out and trampled underfoot." (Mt. 5:13)

The children of Jacob were to be set apart, to be *in* the land but not *of* the land. To be in the world, but not of the world. They were to live in the land, in the world, but to find their identity and calling as those belonging to the Lord and not from anywhere else. They were to live lives that pointed others to God. The path of Esau is a path where that distinctive identity and calling is lost, where the church fades into just another social program, into just another personal preference in a world filled to the brim with choices. The path of Esau in Genesis 36 is the path of assimilation and compromise. Esau is the child of Abraham who has lost who he is. Genesis 36 is here in the Bible, in part, as a warning, so that we would not walk the path of Esau.

Instead, the way forward for us is different than the

path of Esau. The path of faithfulness cannot be to retreat from the world, as tempting as that may be at times. The way forward will be to live *as* God's people. Jacob's descendants were to live out God's will in the midst of the world as witness to God. Christians live as citizens of heaven even as we walk as citizens of various countries throughout this world. The path of faithfulness will be to live by the claims and promise of the gospel even in a world increasingly turned away from God.

The way forward for the church is the same as it was for the descendants of Jacob. It is continually to be called back to our identity and calling as the people of God. We are people called and commissioned by grace, made right with God through the precious blood of his Son, and called to live so that the world may know the LORD. By the gracious hand of God, may our genealogies be written far differently than that of Esau.

The Ghost of Esau Yet to Come: Saul

> "These are the sons of Zibeon: Aiah and Anah, he is the Anah who found the springs in the wilderness as he pastured the donkeys of his father Zibeon" (Genesis 36:24)

The most significant connection in Esau's genealogy is not backward or sideways, but forward. Esau is like Lot, separating from God's people and leading to ruin. He is the child of Abraham that has lost his identity and blended into the nations of the world. But Esau is also King Saul. Perhaps, more accurately, we learn in Genesis 36 that King Saul is a new Esau.

Looking for Donkeys in the Wilderness

There are three different details in the genealogy of Esau

that connect him to Saul. The first is found in a curious detail in Genesis 36:24, "These are the sons of Zibeon: Aiah and Anah, he is the Anah *who found the springs in the wilderness as he pastured the donkeys of his father* Zibeon." There are no wasted words in the Bible. Perhaps Anah was well-known for this incident, but there is a deeper explanation. There are plenty of stories of people pasturing sheep in the wilderness, but there are very few stories involving donkeys. In 1 Samuel 9, Saul's father's donkeys get lost. Saul travels a long distance through the lands of Ephraim, Shalishah, Shaalim, and Benjamin, but cannot find the donkeys. He is about to turn back when the boy who is with him tells him that a man of God is in the town ahead. Along the way, he meets women at a well who direct him to the prophet Samuel. Samuel had been told by the Lord that a man from Benjamin would come that day and Samuel was to anoint him king over Israel. Saul is anointed and the donkeys are proclaimed found.

The placement of this detail regarding donkeys in the wilderness in the genealogy of Esau helps us to see how God wants us to understand not just Esau, but Saul. Saul is an Esau-like character. David and Saul's story runs along the same lines as Jacob and Esau. David is the younger who is chosen by God over Saul. Saul, like Esau with Jacob, desires to kill David, but God protects David. David, like Jacob, has to flee the land and serve foreigners to avoid being killed by Saul.

Agag & Amalek

But the connection runs deeper. There is another name in the genealogy of Esau that connects directly to Saul: Amalek. Genesis 36:12 tells us that "Timna was a concubine to Eliphaz, Esau's son; she bore Amalek to Eliphaz." The descendants of Amalek – the Amalekites – show up at multiple points in the biblical story. The Amalekites attacked and harried Israel when they left Egypt. In 1 Samuel 15, Samuel tells Saul that the Lord has declared judgment on the Amalekites for their treatment of Israel and that Saul is to attack them and destroy them completely. Every single person or animal is to be killed. Saul musters an army and attacks, defeating the Amalekites, but taking their king, Agag, alive as a captive. Contrary to God's command, Saul spares Agag and the best of the sheep and cattle of the Amalekites. This disobedience is pivotal in the reign of Saul, for God says afterward, "I regret that I have made Saul king" (1 Sam 15:11). Amalek is a child of Esau, the son of Abraham who lost his way and his identity. Saul is supposed to wipe them from the earth, but – like Esau before him – he compromises with the people of the land. He refuses God's call to be holy, to be set apart, and this failure eventually leads to the downfall of Saul and will haunt his people for generations.

Agag, the Amalekite, does not go quietly. His name shows up again at another time when the distinctiveness of God's people is in question. In the book of Esther, Mordecai of the tribe of Benjamin (the same tribe as Saul), runs afoul of Haman, a descendant of Agag, the Amalekite (Esther 3:1-2). In response, Haman plots to destroy not just Mordecai, but the entire Jewish people (3:5-6). By the grace of God, through the shrewd wisdom of Esther, Haman's plot turns back upon him and he is killed (7:1-10). Through Amalek, Esau connects to Saul all the way to Esther. Saul follows along the same path as Esau by losing his distinctiveness and setting aside his calling. Esther reverses the path of Esau and Saul by living into her distinctive calling and rescuing her people. She does not set aside her Jewish identity, but risks herself in solidarity with her people.

A King Like the Nations

There is one last connection between Esau and Saul: they are connected to the kings of the nations. After the period of the judges, God raised up the prophet Samuel. Samuel served the Lord and led the people to serve the Lord as well. Throughout his long life, he led the people of Israel. As he grew old, he appointed his two sons – Joel and Abijah – to serve as leaders. However, these sons did not walk in the Lord's ways. "They turned aside after dishonest gain and accepted bribes and perverted justice" (1 Sam 8:3). So the elders of Israel came to Samuel to ask for a king. In their request were two contradictory desires. They wanted a king because Samuel's sons did not follow God's ways. "You are old, and your sons do not follow your ways" (1 Sam 8:5). They had leaders who dishonored God through their leadership and would inevitably lead the people astray. They wanted a leader who would be different, who would help them to walk in God's ways, unlike Samuel's sons, Joel and Abijah.

Yet, there was a second reason for asking for a king: they wanted to be like every other nation. They said to Samuel, "Now appoint a king to lead us, such as all the other nations have" (1 Sam 8:5). Samuel pointed out just what such a king would do. He will conscript their sons as soldiers, force them to farm the soil for the king and force still others to make weapons. He will take their daughters into his service and take the best of their fields. The king will demand the best of all that they have so that they will eventually cry out to the Lord for relief. Yet, the people's mind remained firm: "But the people refused to listen to Samuel. "No!" they said. "We want a king over us. Then we will be like all the other nations, with a king to lead us and to go out and fight our battles" (1 Sam 8:19-20). Though the Lord reveals that Israel is rejecting Him as their king, He tells Samuel to anoint a king. That king — the one like the nations — is Saul.

Israel wanted a king so that they would not be led astray from the ways of God, but they also wanted a king so they could be just like everyone else. They wanted a "king like the other nations." Despite their requests, they could not have both. Either they would have a king after God's own heart or a king like the other nations. Either they would have a king who would lead them in God's ways and help them to live out their distinctive calling in the world, or they would have a king who would lead them away from God and make them indistinguishable from the rest of the world. One way to read the history of Israel is that the people desperately need the first kind of king — one after God's heart — but what they really wanted most of the time was the second kind — a king like the nations. They needed David, but they really wanted Saul.

In Genesis 36, we see the pattern of Esau tracing down toward the kings of the nations. Esau sells his birthright for a pot of stew, abandons his distinctive calling as a child of Abraham, and become indistinguishable from the nations around him. So much so that the genealogy of Esau contains within it a list of the kings of Edom. Instead of being after God's own heart, Esau chose to be like the nations and the fruit of that is the Edomite kings. However, tucked into that list of kings are two names that deepen this connection between Saul and Esau: Shaul and Baal-Hanan. Shaul is a form of the name Saul. Saul's oldest son was named Jonathan, which means "The LORD is gracious." The king who came after Shaul was named Baal-Hanan, which means "Baal is gracious." The similarity of names and the parallel meaning is striking.

Though not literally the same Saul who was the first king of Israel, the inclusion of Shaul should be like a warning flag for Israel. If we go the way of Esau instead of Jacob, we will end up with Saul instead of David. The result of Esau's path is Shaul and Baal-Hanan. These are worldly kings, kings who demand their rights, who take the best from their people for their own use. They are kings who use their people's labor to fashion weapons of war, not songs of praise to the Lord. When Israel longs for a "king like the other nations," they are walking the path of Esau, not Jacob. When they actually get what they ask for, the result is Saul.

Esau's refusal to take up his birthright and live as a child of Abraham lead to his people being indistinguishable from the nations and lead to the likes of Shaul and Baal-Hanan. In a similar way, when Israel refused to live as God's distinctive people and wanted to be just like all the other nations, it lead to the likes of Saul.

The genealogy of Esau serves as a preview and warning concerning the period of the kings. Though full of names we barely recognize, the genealogy of Esau tells a story. It begins with Esau losing his distinctiveness and joining himself to the nations around him as he married Adah, Oholibamah, and Basemath. The genealogy ends with a certain form of elevation. From Esau comes a line of kings and a series of chiefs. However, that worldly elevation is actually a descent from the glorious calling of the children of Abraham. By the end of the story, Esau is no different than the world around him. He is salt that has lost its saltiness. It is no longer good for anything, but is thrown out and trampled underfoot.

This story repeats itself as Israel demands a king and gets one like the nations — Saul. Though in some ways

Saul's coronation is the culmination of generations of Israel wanting to "do what was right in its own eyes" (Judges 21:25), it is also, in many other ways, the beginning of Israel walking down the path of losing its distinctiveness. In placing Esau's genealogy in the Bible and preserving the connections to the life of Saul, God uses this genealogy to call us to consider the path of Esau and the path of Jacob and where they finally lead.

> "Blessed is the one who does not walk in step with the wicked or stand in the way that sinners take or sit in the company of mockers, but whose delight is in the law of the LORD, and who meditates on his law day and night. That person is like a tree planted by streams of water, which yields its fruit in season and whose leaf does not wither— whatever they do prospers.
> Not so the wicked! They are like chaff that the wind blows away. Therefore the wicked will not stand in the judgment, nor sinners in the assembly of the righteous.
> For the LORD watches over the way of the righteous, but the way of the wicked leads to destruction." (Psalm 1, NIV)

Conclusion

Three ghosts appear to Ebenezer Scrooge during the night as a warning. He is given a glimpse of the past, present, and future in order to call him to consider his life and the consequences of his path. A Christmas Carol is a call to repentance. It is a call for Scrooge to turn from the path he has been treading in order to start down another.

The genealogy of Esau is a similar call to repentance. The genealogy connects backward to Lot, points ahead to

Saul, and calls for Israel in the present to consider its ways. Will it walk the path of Esau or turn toward the path of Jacob? Will it seek to be like the nations or seek to be a people after God's own heart? Esau's genealogy shows the results of one of the paths and serves as a warning for the church as it considers its mission as spiritual children of Abraham.

This exploration is not exhaustive, but just scratches the surface of all the connections. The Edomites draw us to Herod and Jesus. The relationship between the Ishmaelites, Midianites, and Edomites will come back again when Joseph is sold into slavery in Genesis 37. It's all connected and the genealogies highlight the connections and the ways God works in the world so that we can better understand how we are to read these stories in the Bible.

Discussion Questions:

1. How does the connection between Esau and Lot illumine this genealogy? How does it impact how we understand Esau separating from Jacob?

2. How does the connection between Esau and Jacob illumine this genealogy? What danger do the people of Israel face? What about the church?

3. How does Esau prefigure Saul? How are both "like the nations"?

4. How do these various connections serve as a warning to the church?

Family Blessings:
Genesis 46, 48-49

"Better three hours too soon than a minute too late."
— William Shakespeare

Timing can make all the difference in the world. Babe Ruth points his bat toward the outfield, calling the home run before the pitch even comes down the plate. Steph Curry fires off a three point shot and turns his back to the basket and starts heading down the court before the shot even goes in. Either action done a few seconds later — after the shot goes in, after the home run — would not have the same impact.

In a similar way, timing in the Bible can make all the difference in the world. Many genealogies are included throughout the pages of Scripture, but the Spirit placed them carefully. It is not simply the content of the genealogies, but their placement in the Bible that should inform how we read them. This chapter deals with two separate sections toward the end of Genesis. First, in Genesis 46, we will look at two ways this genealogy invites us to love our neighbor, including just where it is placed in the context of Genesis. Next, in Genesis 48-49 (which is not technically a genealogy) we will notice the character of the various blessings given by Jacob to explore what true blessing actually looks like.

Individuals & Families: Genesis 46

> "His sons, and his sons' sons with him, his daughter, and his sons' daughters; all his offspring he brought with him into Egypt" (Genesis 46:7)

God redeems both individuals and families.

Genesis 46 is the last genealogy in the book of Genesis, a book filled with genealogies. Yet, it is not exactly where we would expect to find it. Genesis 36 is the long genealogy of the children of Esau, then Genesis 37 begins: "Jacob settled in the land where his father had lived as an alien, the land of Canaan. This is the story of the family of Jacob" (37:1). After this, there should be a genealogy listing all the sons and daughters of Jacob. That is how it has usually worked in Genesis. Not here. Instead, we have a twenty year saga where the brothers hated Joseph, stripped him, sold him, and tore their family apart. God was with Joseph and, twenty years later, God knits the family back together. Only then, at the end of that story, do we get the list of the children of Jacob. All these children had been born years earlier, but we get their names at the end, because God cares about the family.

It is only when the family is whole again that we hear about the coming generations. God is at work redeeming individuals, but also redeeming families. These seventy names in nineteen verses in Genesis 46 are concrete individuals with their own stories and struggles, but they are also a family. God's promises, redemption, and plan of salvation in this world is for both individuals and families. God is concerned for Imnah, Ishvah, Ishvi and the whole family of Israel.

We see this double concern for families and individuals throughout the Scriptures. God calls Abraham the individual and promises to give him a family. God rescues the whole family of Israel from Egypt through the individuals he calls – Moses and Aaron. God calls individuals to faith and to trust in him, yet calls them to circumcise their children, to mark them as part of the family of God and raise them to know and love the Lord. We see it all down the line – God calls individual judges, prophets, and kings, yet calls them to work for the redemption of the whole family of God. This double concern continues in the New Testament, where Jesus calls the disciples one by one, and yet calls them into the family of God and calls Christians to raise up children in the faith, marking them with the waters and promises of baptism, so that they too would confess faith in Jesus Christ.

When a child is baptized, her parents bring her to the font to be baptized, and hear the promises of God spoken over her: to forgive her sins, to adopt her in the body of Christ, the church, to send the Holy Spirit daily to renew and cleanse her, and to resurrect her to eternal life. Years later, when that child stands up before the gathered people of God to profess her faith in Jesus, God is keeping his promises made to this family all those years ago. A baptized child of the faith standing up and proclaiming faith in Jesus Christ shows that God cares about families. Yet, that child will also stand there as an individual, as one who herself has heard the gospel and responded in faith. She will stand as one who believes not just because it was taught to her or it is what her family believes, but because she herself believes in Jesus Christ — heart and soul. A baptized child proclaiming faith in Jesus Christ shows that God cares about individuals. She matters to God, you matter to God, all people matter to God, not because of what family they are born into, or what advantages or disadvantages they have received, but because of the good news of the gospel, that Jesus Christ died on the cross to save us from our sins. She has a name and it is by her name that God has called her to faith in Christ.

This is part of the beauty and power of this genealogy here in Genesis 46. There are names. Lots of them. Most of them we know nothing about other than that they are here. Yet, the Holy Spirit consider each and every one of them important enough to be included in Scripture. We know nothing about Muppim, Huppim, and Ard, but God does. It was his will that their names be included here. When the roll call of the family of God is called, they are included. We know nothing about Eri, Arodi, and Areli, but God does. Each individual named in this genealogy is a life that matters to God, even if we know nothing about it.

So if you feel insignificant, like you are nothing but a name on a page, swallowed up by your family or lost in the shuffle, God knows you. Even if no one else does. Even if no one else will remember your name or your story in fifty years, God knows you, just as he knows Jemuel, Jamin, Ohad, Jachin, Zohar, and Shaul.

In the inclusion of this genealogy in Genesis 46, we see God's passion for families and we see God's passion for each and every individual. God's care for individuals and families should shape how Christians love their neighbor.

God loves individuals and families. If God is so concerned about families and individuals, we should be too. If God worked twenty years to knit back together what the brothers had torn apart, making it somehow better than when it started, then Christians should be concerned to strengthen, heal, and knit together families. If God cares about the broken family of Jacob, about the hatred, the lies, and the guilt that threaten to bury them – to the point that he would do all that work through Joseph in Egypt – then we – as followers of Christ – should care for the broken families in our communities, for the hatred, lies, and guilt that threaten to bury them as well. God cares about individuals and families, and if God is so concerned, so should we be.

If God cares for the forgotten names and lives of Ziphion, Haggi, and Shuni, then we should be caring for the nameless and forgotten in our community, those who feel unloved and uncared for as individuals. Learn the names of our neighbors, learn their stories.

Genesis 46 should lead us to love our neighbor more: God's concern for families and individuals should lead us to do the same.

Distinct People of God: Genesis 46

Genesis 46 should also lead us to love our neighbor by being distinct as the people of God. The people of Israel were shepherds. In Genesis 46:31-34, though Joseph wants them to come to eat and be settled in the land of Egypt, he does not tell them to hide their calling and occupation. Instead, they are to be upfront about it, even though it will make them abhorrent to the Egyptians. We do not know whether Joseph does this intentionally or if it is just divine providence, but, by being honest about their calling as shepherds, the Israelites will live *with* the Egyptians, but also *separate* from them. They live among the Egyptians, but never as one of them. Unlike Esau, whose descendants become indistinguishable from the people of the land, Israel remains distinct during their 430 years in Egypt. This witness will be powerful over the generations they are in Egypt. When God finally brings them out, though Pharaoh and his officials hate and fear them, some of the Egyptians will leave and go with the Israelites out of Egypt (Ex. 12: 38).

One of the ways we love our neighbor by being distinct as the people of God. We have been called to a different way of life than the way of the world. We have been called to follow Jesus — loving enemies, turning the other cheek, forgiving seventy-seven times, rooting out lust, not worshipping money. We have been called to live differently. Like the sons of Israel, that will mean living in the Egypt, but never belonging to Egypt, living in the world but never belonging to it. In the same way, living for Christ — even if it is abhorrent to the world — is one of the best ways we love our neighbors.

The Blessing of Jacob: Genesis 48-49

Genesis 46 is placed at the end of the story of Joseph and his brothers to demonstrate God's will to redeem both individuals and families. It is only after the family is whole again that they are listed together with all their children and grandchildren. Yet, even in that listing, they are called to be set apart as God's people. These themes of family and calling are carried forward during the blessings that Jacob pronounces over his children.

What does blessing look like? Genesis 48 and 49 is full of blessings. Jacob tells of God's blessing at Luz. Jacob blesses Ephraim and Manasseh, then his twelve sons. Blessing after blessing. Yet, if we are honest, a lot of this doesn't look much like blessing to us. Instead of a warm and fuzzy feeling — something that seems and feels obviously good — we have harsh words of judgment. Instead of being told to "be true to yourself," the sons are given painfully honest words about their character. Instead of miracle cures and overflowing prosperity, we have strength in the midst of trials. It doesn't quite look like blessing to us.

Yet, throughout these two chapters, the words of Jacob are called "blessing" and when the whole section is summed up in Genesis 49:28, we are told, "this is what their father said to them when he blessed them, blessing each one of them with a suitable blessing." Perhaps the problem is not with the blessings, but with our understanding of what it means to be blessed. Perhaps blessing is harder and better than we might imagine.

THE BLESSING OF JUDGMENT

Sometimes blessing is the gift of judgment. This judgment can be a blessing because it forces us to confront our sin.

Jacob gives a suitable blessing to each one of his sons and those blessings include judgment. Reuben, the first born, was the oldest, the strongest, and should have been the leader of his brothers. Yet, Reuben's character is unstable. Years ago, back in Genesis 35, Reuben had slept with Bilhah, his father's concubine. At the time, Jacob said nothing. But decades passed and the sin had not been dealt with and it results in judgment upon Reuben. Reuben is removed from his firstborn position among the brothers:

> "Unstable as water, you shall no longer excel because you went up onto your father's bed; then you defiled it – you went up onto my couch!" (Gen. 49:4)

To our knowledge, none of the leaders in Israel's history ever come from the line of Reuben.

Then Jacob moves to Simeon and Levi. After Dinah was raped at Shechem (Genesis 34), Simeon and Levi agreed to let the men of Shechem join with the people of Israel as long as they were circumcised. The Shechemites agreed and while they were recovering, Simeon and Levi went in and slaughtered the whole city in retribution for what happened to Dinah. Again, this unreconciled sin returns upon the brothers:

> "for in their anger they killed men, and at their whim they hamstrung oxen. Cursed be their anger, for it is fierce, and their wrath, for it is cruel! I will divide them in Jacob and scatter them in Israel." (Gen. 49:6-7)

When the family leaves Egypt and finally enters the promised land, the lands of Simeon are divided within the land of Judah. As the priests of God, the Levites are given specific cities through the land of Israel. They are scattered among the people. The Levites later found favor in God's sight by their courage in confronting sin (Ex. 32:25-29). This earned them the role as priests in the house of God and shows they may have listened to what Jacob said. They turned their anger from fierce cruelty into zeal for God.

We also see lesser judgments in the blessings of Isaachar, Dan, Gad, and Benjamin. Each statement of character is an invitation to take a hard look at themselves and their own sinful tendencies. The history of Israel bears the truth of the words of Jacob – Benjamin does devour and divide (Gen. 49:27). Dan is a snake (49:17). Gad is raided frequently (49:19). Isaachar was given good land without having to struggle for it (49:15). Yet, while this should give us confidence in the reliability of God's Word, we should not view it fatalistically. The blessings on the brothers were honest evaluations of their character, which is a form of judgment that is also a blessing. It invites us to see ourselves truly and then turn toward the Lord.

These blessings don't look like blessings to us. Yet, judgment can be a blessing when it forces us to confront our sins. Reuben, Simeon, and Levi — and their descendants after them — would have heard this blessing often. They would have been regularly reminded of the sins of their fathers. As hard as this might have been, it was an invitation to repentance and to walk in a different way. If sin is not dealt with by confession and repentance — in individuals or in family — it will catch up with us eventually. Judgment can be a blessing when it invites us to confront our own sin.

We don't know how these blessings changed Reuben and Simeon and their families. But we do see in Levi that the anger and wrath which was cursed here in Genesis, will become an instrument of passion for God by the time of the Exodus. Sometimes blessing is the gift of judgment. This judgment can be a blessing because it forces us to confront our sin.

The Blessing of Strength

However, sometimes blessing is the gift of strength. Sometimes that strength is unexpected blessing. Ephraim receives the right hand of blessing – the greater blessing – even though he is the younger of his brothers (Gen. 48:14). God has a beautiful habit of surprising us in who he chooses to bless. Yet, the strength God promises often comes in the midst of trials and hardship. We see this in both Judah and Joseph. The blessings on these two sons are longer and look more obviously like blessings. Judah will be praised by his brothers, he will have rule and power, tribute and obedience (Gen. 49:8-10). Joseph is a fruitful bough whose branches run over the wall. He will have blessing from God – from heaven, from the deep, from the breast, from the womb (Gen. 49:22-26).

Yet, when Jacob gives these blessings, he also promises trials. God's blessing will be strength in the midst of these trials. Judah will have his hand on the neck of his enemies (49:8), but that means that Judah will have enemies. God's blessing does not mean life will be easy, that there will be no struggle, that life is all smooth sailing and calm seas. Instead, God promises him strength in the midst of the fight. Joseph will be attacked:

> "The archers fiercely attacked him; they shot at him and pressed him hard. Yet his bow remained taut, and his arms were made agile by the hands of the Mighty One of Jacob." (49:23-24)

Being blessed by God doesn't exclude being shot at, being attacked, being pressed hard. This was Joseph's life as the blessed of God. Yet, God's promise through Jacob was that God's hand would strengthen his arms in the struggle. Though he is weary from the fight, his strength will not give way.

This is the blessing of God — strength in the midst of trial. This is good news for all of us whose life does not look blessed right now. For families that are feeling empty and dry, for when the struggle never seems to end and you feel like you are just taking one arrow after another. For those of us who wake up every day wondering if our arms will finally give out under this load. The promise of God is not that there will be no trials, but that God will be with you in them.

The archers fiercely attacked him; they shot at him and pressed him hard. Yet his bow remained taut, and his arms were made agile by the hands of the Mighty One of Jacob, by the name of the Shepherd, the Rock of Israel, by the God of your father, who will be with you, by the Almighty who will bless you with blessings of heaven above blessings of the deep that lies beneath, blessings of the breast and of the womb. (49:23-25)

In Judah and Joseph, we see God promising strength, not to avoid trials and hardship, but in the midst of them. For those of us walking in the way of Jesus, God's blessing may often look like the gift of strength.

The Blessing of Promise

Lastly, we see in Genesis 48 and 49 that sometimes blessing is the gift of the promise. These blessings are sometimes invitations to confront our sins and walk in holiness, they are sometimes comfort and strength in the midst of trial, but they are also promises of the future. All the way back in Genesis, back when Israel first entered Egypt, God made a promise to Judah through the lips of his father, Jacob:

> The scepter shall not depart from Judah, nor the ruler's staff from between his feet, until tribute comes to him; and the obedience of the peoples is his. Binding his foal to the vine and his donkey's colt to the choice vine, he washes his garments in wine and his robe in the blood of grapes; his eyes are darker than wine, and his teeth whiter than milk. (49:10-12)

Centuries in Egypt left the people meditating on these

words, and then centuries with no king, only judges and prophets. When Israel finally gets a king, God gives them a king like the nations — Saul the Benjaminite — a ravenous wolf of a man. But then the Lord selects a young shepherd boy from Bethlehem, a son of Judah. David is anointed king. He takes up the scepter and the ruler's staff and God promises that a Son of David will remain on God's throne forever — a promise echoing back here to Genesis, where the ruler's staff will not depart from between Judah's feet. But the failure of the sons of David to live up to their calling stirs the hope that the promise to David, the promise to Judah back here on the lips of Jacob spoke to something greater, some*one* greater. By the words of the prophets, the Spirit revealed that they were not waiting for just a son of David, but *the* Son of David. And then Zechariah picked up the imagery of Genesis 49 when he says,

> Rejoice greatly, Daughter Zion!
> Shout, Daughter Jerusalem!
> See, your king comes to you,
> righteous and victorious,
> lowly and riding on a donkey,
> on a colt, the foal of a donkey. (Zech 9:9)

A foal, a donkey's colt, were the signs of the king who is coming, the son of Judah, the son of David. Then Jesus, a week before he would die and rise again for us and for our salvation, went to enter Jerusalem.

> "As they approached Jerusalem and came to Bethphage on the Mount of Olives, Jesus sent two disciples, saying to them, "Go to the village ahead of you, and at once you will find a donkey tied there, with her colt by her. Untie them and bring them to me. If anyone says

anything to you, say that the Lord needs them, and he will send them right away."

This took place to fulfill what was spoken through the prophet:
"Say to Daughter Zion,
'See, your king comes to you,
gentle and riding on a donkey,
and on a colt, the foal of a donkey.'"

The disciples went and did as Jesus had instructed them. They brought the donkey and the colt and placed their cloaks on them for Jesus to sit on. A very large crowd spread their cloaks on the road, while others cut branches from the trees and spread them on the road. The crowds that went ahead of him and those that followed shouted,
"Hosanna to the Son of David!"
"Blessed is he who comes in the name of the Lord!"
"Hosanna in the highest heaven!" (Matt 21:1-9)

Sometimes blessing is the gift of the promise. When Jacob speaks a blessing over Judah, his words echo down the chambers of time through Zechariah until they reach their resounding crescendo in the coming of Jesus. Jacob promises Jesus. All those years ago, God had already purposed and promised to send his Son, born of Judah, for the sake of the world. The prophecy was fulfilled, the promised blessings of God did come. They came in Jesus Christ.

What does it look like to be blessed? The blessing of God often looks different than what the world counts as blessed. It can sometimes look like judgment that forces us to confront our sin and turn to Christ. It can sometimes look like strength in the midst of trials and hardships. And it looks like Jesus, the son of Judah, riding on a foal, on the colt of a donkey.

Conclusion

Timing can make all the difference in the world. Genesis 46 is placed at the end of the story of Joseph, showing God's restoration and healing of the family of Jacob. The series of blessings Jacob pronounces upon his children will force some to confront their sins, give others strength in the midst of trials, but also ultimately point to a future where Jesus is the fulfillment of the promise to Judah. It is not only the content of the genealogies, but where they are placed in the Bible that can help us read them more beneficially.

Discussion Questions:

1. How do we see God's concern for families in the story of Joseph? Where else do we see this in the Bible?

2. How do we see God's concern for individuals in the story of Joseph? Where else do we see this in the Bible?

3. What do we typically think it looks like to be "blessed"? How does Jacob's blessing of his sons change how we view blessing?

Radical Faith & Ordinary Faithfulness:

Ruth 4

"They named him Obed; he became the father of Jesse, the father of David." – Ruth 4:17

We may never know the full impact of ordinary faithfulness. The genealogy at the end of the book of Ruth is one of the shortest in the whole Bible. It is only five or six verses long (depending on how you count it). It only has ten names. Yet its placement at the end of the book drastically changes how we read the entire story of Ruth. By including this genealogy, what might have looked like it was simply one small story of a family struggling through famine is drawn into the larger story of God's redemption of the world.

From Empty to Full

The book of Ruth ends with the birth of a child, Obed. "The women of the neighborhood gave him a name, saying, "A son has been born to Naomi." They named him Obed; he became the father of Jesse, the father of David" (4:17). It's an ending for Ruth and Naomi that a few months earlier would have seemed impossible.

The book of Ruth begins with a famine. It was the period of the judges, when "everyone did what was right in their own eyes" (Judges 21:25). A famine strikes Bethlehem (whose name literally means "the house of bread") and the food is gone. Elimelech, his wife Naomi, and their two sons, Mahlon and Chilion, all leave the land of Israel and head to the land of Moab. Ten years in Moab and Naomi watches first her husband, then one son and then another wither like dry grass and die. All that is left is her two Moabite daughters-in-law, freshly widowed. These three women are vulnerable and empty. Naomi seeks to send them away, back to their families. One daughter-in-law, Orpah, eventually relents and leaves. However, the other, Ruth, refuses to leave her mother-in-law's side. "But Ruth said, "Do not press me to leave you or to turn back from following you! Where you go, I will go; where you lodge, I will lodge; your people shall be my people, and your God my God. Where you die, I will die — there will I be buried. May the LORD do thus and so to me, and more as well, if even death parts me from you" (Ruth 1:16-17 NRSV). So the two women journey back to Bethlehem together, still empty.

The story of Ruth is one of incredible faith and ordinary faithfulness. Ruth leaves land and gods behind to cling to Naomi and to the God Naomi serves. This is incredible faith. Yet, much of the activity in the book is fairly ordinary. The women have no means of providing for themselves, so Ruth goes to glean in the fields. She plans to pick up the leftover grain that falls to the ground after the workers have gone through to harvest. An upstanding man, Boaz, sees her and asks about her situation. Once he learns of her plight, Boaz instructs his workers to leave behind extra grain for Ruth to gather, ensuring she and Naomi will have enough to eat.

When Ruth returns home with a sack full of grain, Naomi learns of Boaz. Not only is he a good man, but he is a near relative. In the Bible, it was the nearest relatives who were responsible for caring for the widows in a family, including potentially marrying them and having children to continue the name of the dead husband. Naomi has Ruth go to Boaz in the night and plead for protection. Boaz promises he will do all he can, but that there is another relative nearer in relation than him. The very next morning, Boaz confronts this man (whose name is never given) at the gate of the city. When the man refuses to take up his responsibility as a "kinsman-redeemer," Boaz takes up the mantle. He marries Ruth and they have a son, Obed.

It is a story of incredible faith and ordinary faithfulness. Naomi returns home to a people where she has no place, to land that hasn't been worked for ten years, with another mouth to feed. Her life is empty.

Her house was empty, her cupboards were empty, her hopes seemed empty, and yet – a child was born in Bethlehem, and the women said, "Praise be to the Lord." And now a grandson is sitting on Naomi's lap, wrapped in Naomi's arms. That grandson was a sign that the emptiness she felt has been replaced by fullness through God's grace.

What was empty is now full. The home, the cupboards, the future, all filled to the brim. This is God's grace to Naomi and Ruth. Through the love and compassion of Boaz, two women who held on to the Lord found their emptiness filled, their sorrow turned to joy, and their bitterness turned to praise. What had looked like a dead end was now overflowing with life. God was faithful, using the faithfulness of an ordinary man like Boaz to bless two poor widows and restore a family. The change from the end of the first chapter to the end of the story is astounding and we can see God's redemptive work.

This full ending begins to overflow with the genealogy tucked in at the end. This child of Ruth who sits on Naomi's lap is the grandfather of King David. God's gracious provision in the midst of ordinary faithfulness is connected into the larger story of God's redemption, because this genealogy connects Ruth's story to the story of David.

Surprise Inclusion: Ruth, Rahab, and Tamar

The genealogy of Obed is a narrowing genealogy. The genealogy's point comes at the end, in the person of David. It also follows a family through one son after another, not mentioning the whole family. In short, the genealogy is meant to emphasize the fulfillment and carrying forward of God's promise in the person of David. This story of ordinary faithfulness is caught up in the larger story of salvation.

However, this genealogy is also scandalous. This connection to David underscores the radical inclusion of Ruth into the story of God's redemption. Ruth was a Moabitess. She was born a national and religious outsider. She worshipped other gods and her people were no friends to Israel. Even greater, her people were barred from entering the sanctuary of God. "No Ammonite or Moabite or any of their descendants may enter the assembly of the LORD, not even in the tenth generation." (Dt. 23:3). David is only three generations removed from Ruth. Yet, Ruth came to God in genuine and heartfelt faith and was graciously included in the covenant people. Her story was recorded and placed in the Scriptures. Though she began outside, she was welcomed in through faith. The genealogy in Ruth also includes Perez, who was the son of Tamar and Judah (Gen 46:12). Tamar was also not originally from the people of God. Yet, she is included in the story. Salmon, who is mentioned as the father of Boaz, had married Rahab, the harlot from Jericho. Another outsider who is brought in. This short genealogy of David at the end of Ruth shows God's radical inclusion of the outsider. It demonstrates the place of radical faith and ordinary faithfulness when these people are drawn into the larger story of God's work. The story of Ruth has shown how a Moabite woman obtained an exalted place in Hebrew history. There is later evidence that David did not forget his Moabite roots. During the period of flight from Saul's wrath, David asked the king of Moab to let his parents stay there for refuge (1 Sam. 22:3-4).

In Ruth, God fills what is empty. This is not just about Ruth and Naomi, but about David and Israel. Through David, the grandson of Ruth, God fills up the house of Israel. Through David, we see radical faith and ordinary faithfulness. Through David, the covenant of redemption is narrowed to this son of Jesse and his descendants. Ultimately, the genealogy of Ruth connects us all the way to Jesus, the Son of David. Through Jesus, the outsider leaves behind an old life and is welcomed into the covenant by grace, just like Ruth. Through Jesus, we are called to radical faith in Jesus and called to ordinary faithfulness to God. Through Jesus, the covenant is narrowed to one man, and yet expanded to the whole world through faith in him.

God's hand is at work in the ordinary days of history. Two people — Ruth and Boaz — are brought together by a highly unlikely series of circumstances and become ancestors of the great king of Israel — David — and provide a link to the Messiah, Jesus.

The Impact of Ordinary Faithfulness

As it turns out, this story is much bigger than two widows and a farmer. The story of God bringing fullness to these two women is part of an even bigger drama that none of them could see. Ruth and Boaz were King David's great-grandparents, which also means they are in the family line of Jesus.

There is no way Ruth and Boaz would have known the impact of their faith in God. They could not have known how God would use their ordinary life of faith for his mission. Yet through the faithfulness of these ordinary people, God prepared the way for incredible things.

Like Ruth and Boaz, we don't know what future impact our faithfulness will have. We don't know what God will do with our emptying of ourselves for the sake of others.

But we do know that, like Ruth and Boaz, God will use our ordinary faithfulness for his glory.

Discussion Questions:

1. How does God use "ordinary faithfulness" in the life of Ruth, Naomi, and Boaz? How have you see God use people's ordinary faithfulness in your life?

2. Why is it surprising that Ruth ends with David? Why is this ending important for understanding the whole book of Ruth?

Breathing with Both Lungs:

Matthew 1:1-18

"An account of the genealogy of Jesus the Messiah, the son of David, the son of Abraham." – Matthew 1:1

Take a deep breath. As the air enters your nose or mouth, it passes down into your trachea before branching and filling both your lungs. It is part of God's design that we have two lungs for breathing. Oxygen enters your blood through your lungs, enabling you to run, jump, dance, think, and live in all the ways we do. While it is possible to live with only one functioning lung, it can be difficult. Even if all the other parts of your body function well, your capacity is limited because you cannot get as much oxygen to the rest of your body. We were made to breathe with two lungs, not just one.

For a long time, many Christians have been breathing with only one lung. God has given us two testaments — Old and New — by which to know him, know his ways, and know his salvation. We are meant to breathe with both lungs — to draw in the life-giving Spirit from both testaments. The Old and New Testaments together are one book, just as our two lungs are one respiratory system. However, many of us read the Bible as if we should only breathe with one lung at a time. Those couple pages in the middle of our Bibles that separate the Old and New Testaments can feel like a dividing wall.

However, the genealogy at the opening of Matthew is a reminder to breathe with both lungs. Jesus' genealogy draws the Old and New Testaments together into one book. There is no such thing as a "New Testament Christian," for when we open the New Testament, the first words we see are "An account of the genealogy of Jesus the Messiah, the son of David, the son of Abraham" (Mt. 1:1). Jesus' identity is connected to the stories and identity of Abraham and David. As the sinews of Scripture, this genealogy connects the two great halves of Scripture, the two lungs of the Word, so that we can breathe deeply and fully.

As we learn to breathe with both lungs, there are two sets of details in this genealogy that deserve our attention. First, Jesus is given three titles in the opening verse of Matthew: Messiah, Son of Abraham, and Son of David. Each of these titles reveals Jesus' identity and calling. Second, this genealogy of Jesus is divided into three sets of fourteen generations. Each third of the genealogy also helps us see the connections between the larger story of Scripture and the person and work of Jesus. Our exploration of this genealogy will be structured around these two sets of details.

Messiah, Son of David, Son of Abraham: Who is Jesus?

Son of Abraham

Jesus is the son of Abraham. He is the child of promise, born to save. When God's good world fell into sin through the disobedience of our first parents, Adam and Eve, God promised that a child of Eve would one day crush the head of the serpent that had deceived them (Gen. 3:15). God promised a child of Eve would be born to save. The world and humanity spiraled down and away from God and God called one man and made him a promise. God called Abram, later renaming him Abraham, and promised to be his God and Abraham and his descendants would be God's people. God's redemption would come through Abraham and his children. God said, "I will make of you a great nation, and I will bless you, and make your name great, so that you will be a blessing. I will bless those who bless you, and the one who curses you I will curse, and in you all the families of the earth will be blessed" (Genesis 12:2-3). God promised Abraham a child through whom God's blessing would come to all the families of the earth. God established his relationship with Abraham, a covenant, and promised to be his God and the God of his children forever (Genesis 17). God even promised to rescue and redeem them from bondage. If they were to break their relationship with God, God himself would pay the cost to restore their relationship (Genesis 15). All of that is wrapped up in God's promise of a child. Through this child of Abraham, God would save and bring blessing to the whole world.

That promise was carried by Abraham's son, Isaac, but he was not the child born to save and bless. The promise was carried by his son, Jacob, too. He was not the child either. Generation after generation, the promise continued but the child did not come. Judah, Perez, Hezron, Aram, Aminadab. Generations of waiting for the child God promised, the child born to save and to bless. Generations waiting, until Jesus. Verse 1 of Matthew 1 and the following genealogy is not simply the proclamation that Jesus is *a* son of Abraham, but that he was *the* son of Abraham. He is *the* child God promised long ago, the one born to save and to bless. By giving us this genealogy, Matthew is telling us the identity of Jesus. He is the Son of Abraham, the child God promised would bring blessing to all the families of the earth, who would save and redeem God's people, who would crush the head of the serpent.

Son of David

Matthew 1 also proclaims that Jesus is the son of David. If the Son of Abraham is the promised Savior, the Son of David is the promised Lord or King. God made a promise to David is 2 Samuel chapter 7:

> "'The Lord declares to you that the Lord himself will establish a house for you: When your days are over and you rest with your ancestors, I will raise up your offspring to succeed you, your own flesh and blood, and I will establish his kingdom. He is the one who will build a house for my Name, and I will establish the throne of his kingdom forever. I will be his father, and he will be my son. When he does wrong, I will punish him with a rod wielded by men, with floggings inflicted by human hands. But my love will never be taken away from him, as I took it away from Saul, whom I removed from before you. Your house and your

kingdom will endure forever before me; your throne will be established forever.'" (2 Sam. 7:11b-16)

The son of David would be called God's Son and God will establish his kingdom and his throne. This Son of David will build a house for the name of the Lord and have a kingdom that will endure forever. God's Son, the true King, will rule with strength and gentleness, justice and compassion, wisdom, mercy, and righteousness. God promised *the* Son of David would one day come who would be the true Lord. For generations, they waited. Many sons of David were born, ruled upon the throne, and died. Good kings and bad kings. Solomon, Hezekiah, Josiah. Uzziah and Ahaz. Their kingdoms ended. They did not rule in righteousness. They were sons of David, but none were *the* son of David.

Until Jesus.

Like with the title "Son of Abraham," Matthew 1 calling Jesus "Son of David" is telling us more than that Jesus was a descendant of David, as important as that was. No, we are being told that he is *the* Son of David. He is the promised King who would reign forever and be God's Son. He is the Messiah. The Greek word *Christ* and the Hebrew word *Messiah* mean the same thing — anointed one. In the Bible, prophets, priests, and kings were anointed as part of being ordained and installed into their positions within God's people. Jesus is the *Messiah*, the *Christ*, the anointed one who was the promised King, the promised Son of David.

THE MESSIAH

While "Messiah" was a title for the Son of David, Jesus is also named specifically as the Messiah. As the Messiah, Jesus comes not in power or prestige, but in humility. Jesus is born only after the fourteen generations of lowliness, obscurity, and humility.

There are a lot of names in Matthew 1. Some of the people named in Jesus' lineage are major characters in the Bible. Abraham, Isaac, Jacob, Judah, and his brothers take up all of Genesis 12 through Genesis 50. Rahab is in the opening chapters of Joshua. Ruth and Boaz have a whole book with their story. David gets multiple books (1-2 Samuel) and wrote a lot of the psalms. Solomon wrote books and there are chapters on his life. Even the more obscure kings in this list still have sections of the Bible devoted to their reigns. Hezekiah and Josiah in particular get quite a bit of treatment in the Bible because they were faithful. Zerubbabel was governor when the people returned to Jerusalem after the exile. But then, nothing. Literally, nothing. We have names in the genealogy here that we know nothing about outside of these few verses. Who was Abiud? Azor? Achim? Joseph's grandfather Matthan? They could have been wonderful, faithful, godly men and fathers, but we know nothing about them. They were obscure.

In the time of Abraham and the patriarchs, God's people were people of promise, sojourners in the land. In the time of David and the kings, they had power and prestige. The Messiah is born only after the people are humbled and obscure, forgotten to the annals of history. Jesus is born in obscurity, lowliness, meekness, and humility.

Matthew begins with "An account of the genealogy of Jesus the Messiah, the son of David, the son of Abraham" (1:1). This is who Jesus is – the child born of Mary. Jesus is the Messiah, born to save and to bless. He is the promised son of Abraham. He is the child of Eve who crushes the head of the serpent and rescues the people from bondage.

He rescues not only from physical bondage, but from the greater bondage to sin, death, and the devil. Jesus is God himself come to pay the penalty for our broken relationship with God. Jesus is God himself come to pour out his life and then pour out the blessing of salvation upon the nations of the earth. Jesus is the promised Son of Abraham who was born to save and to bless. He is the Savior.

Jesus is also the Son of David, the Messiah. He keeps God's law completely and wisdom continually falls forth from his lips. He is the Lord who rules over the church and is putting all his enemies under his feet (Ps. 110). His Word is law and his Word is good. His words are trustworthy and true and authoritative. As Savior, Jesus came to rescue us from our sins. As Lord, Jesus has the authority to direct our life along his paths and not our own. As the Son of Abraham, Jesus redeems us. As the Son of David, he rules over our life.

The genealogy of Jesus holds these two realities together. Jesus is Savior and Lord. Tied up in all the promises to Abraham is a child who would bless and a God who would save. Tied together with all the promises to David is a son who would be God's son and who would rule forever. Jesus is the Son of Abraham and the Son of David. We cannot have one without the other. We cannot have Jesus as the wise sage, lawgiver, or teacher — a New Solomon full of proverbs, parables, and wisdom — and not also have him as the one who saves. We also cannot have Jesus as the Savior and Redeemer without also having him as the Lord who rules our life. He is Savior and Lord.

Yet, when Jesus comes, he comes in humility. He comes out of the family of Achim, Eliud, and Eleazar. He comes in humility and lowliness. This speaks to *how* Jesus is Savior and Lord. He saves and rules, not with power and force, but with suffering humility. Jesus comes as the Messiah, not in the way of glory, but in the lowly way of the cross. It is not only important to know *what* the Messiah came to do, but *how* he did it. Jesus came as Savior and Lord, as Son of Abraham and Son of David, but he came in humility. As Paul says of Jesus,

> "Who, being in very nature God, did not consider equality with God something to be used to his own advantage; rather, he made himself nothing by taking the very nature of a servant, being made in human likeness.
>
> And being found in appearance as a man, he humbled himself by becoming obedient to death—even death on a cross!" (Philippians 2:6-8)

THREE SETS OF FOURTEEN: THE STRUCTURE OF THE GENEALOGY OF JESUS

> "So all the generations from Abraham to David are fourteen generations; and from David to the deportation to Babylon, fourteen generations; and from the deportation to Babylon to the Messiah, fourteen generations." (Matthew 1:17-18)

At the beginning of Matthew 1, we are given three clear titles for Jesus: Son of Abraham, Son of David, Messiah. However, at the end, we are also told that this genealogy divides neatly into three sections of fourteen generations: from Abraham to David, from David to the exile, and from the exile to Jesus. Each of these three sections connects a piece of the Old Testament story into the life of Jesus.

God's Mercy

The first third of Jesus' genealogy, from Abraham through David, reveals God's mercy by who it includes. Matthew includes four women to show the width and depth of the mercy of God.

At the time of Jesus, Jewish ancestry and inheritance was traced through your father — adopted or biological. It was what is known as a patrilineal society. That is why we see "Abraham was the father of Isaac, the father of Jacob, the father of Judah," (Mt. 1:2) and so on. Unsurprisingly, women are not regularly included in a genealogy. When women were mentioned, it was often to emphasize the purity of one's ancestry and the dignity of your family. In a genealogy, you wanted to be able to trace your ancestry back to emphasize the importance of the people you came from.

If someone wants to be king, they need to have clear records of their parents, grandparents, and great-grandparents. Their lineage is vital for their claim to the throne. This is particularly true of a genealogy of someone claiming to be the Messiah, the promised son of Abraham and David. Proving your ancestry is crucial.

However, God is doing something more than simply shoring up Jesus' claim to be Messiah. Matthew includes Tamar in Jesus' genealogy. Tamar married two of Judah's sons, both of whom died as a result of God's judgment (Gen. 38:6-10). Fearing for the life of his third son, Judah refuses to let Tamar marry him (38:11). So Tamar dresses up like a prostitute, meets with Judah, sleeps with him, gets pregnant, and then reveals the whole charade to the community to shame Judah into marrying her and protecting her and her child. Tamar is named in the genealogy of Jesus.

Matthew also includes Rahab. She was a Jerichoite, not an Israelite. She was a prostitute who sheltered the spies of Israel when they went to check out Jericho (Joshua 2). For her kindness, she and her family were spared in the destruction of Jericho. Rahab is in the genealogy of Jesus.

Matthew also includes Ruth. Ruth was a Moabite and a widow. She was taken under the protection of Boaz and married him. Moabites were not allowed to enter the sanctuary of the LORD for ten generations (Dt. 23:3), but Ruth the Moabite is listed as the great-grandmother of David.

Finally, Matthew includes Bathsheba. Well, he includes "Uriah's wife," whom we know to be Bathsheba (2 Sam. 11:3). Bathsheba was, by marriage, a Hittite and the victim of David's adulterous seduction and widowed by his murderous cover-up. Yet, Bathsheba is in the genealogy of Jesus.

The inclusion of these four women in the genealogy of Jesus is shockingly gracious. Each of these four women were ethnic outsiders. They were foreigners, aliens, vulnerable, and easily marginalized, but the story of the Messiah's coming includes them. They belong to the family of Jesus. Three of them were widows — weak and vulnerable in a society where one's attachment to a husband or father was the only source of provision and protection. The inclusion of these women shows how wide God's mercy is. Already, the family of Jesus includes Gentiles.

God promised through Abraham that *all* the nations would be blessed. Jesus came as the Messiah not just for Israel, but for all the nations. We see this already in Jesus' genealogy. The outsiders are included. God's mercy is for all the nations. The coming of the Messiah for the inclusion of the Gentiles is foreshadowed in Jesus' family tree.

God's mercy is also deep. This inclusion of these women is not only about ethnic and religious outsiders, but moral outsiders as well. Each of them were sinners. The men are no better. In two of the stories — Judah and Tamar and David and Bathsheba — the men are clearly the villains according to the Bible. Yet, they are all including in the story of the coming of Jesus Christ.

God's mercy is deep enough to forgive sinners and wide enough to include outsiders. So hear the good news: Jesus came into this world to bring mercy to Judah and Tamar, Rahab, Ruth and Boaz, David and Bathsheba, you and me. No one is too far outside that they cannot come in. No sin is too deep that cannot be forgiven. This is the wide and deep mercy of God.

God's Judgment

The second third of the genealogy of Jesus — from David to the exile to Babylon — reveals God's judgment by what is changed and what is removed from the genealogy. If David was the peak of Israel's kingship — David, the man after God's own heart — then the exile was the darkest valley. This section of the genealogy ends in judgment, but how Matthew handles it also reveals God's judgment upon the people of God both for their unfaithfulness to him and for their lack of mercy toward others.

God's judgment in this section is easier to see when we know the story really well. Some of us had to memorize the list of presidents in school. In a similar way, many Israelites knew the list of the names of the kings of Judah. When Matthew removes several names, they would notice. Between Jehoram and Uzziah, Matthew removes three kings and between Josiah and Jeconiah he cuts out

Jehoiakim. It could be that Matthew is trying to pare down the list to get fourteen names for the sake of symmetry, but there might be more going on. The inclusion of the four women in the first section reveals God's mercy toward sinners and outsiders, his radical inclusion of those we would not expect to find listed in the people of God. In a similar way, the removal of those we might expect to find reveals God's judgment. Four unexpected outsiders are included, but four expected kings are excluded. Those who expected to be insiders and yet continued to walk in darkness can find their names not written in the book. God not only forgives, he also demands. We cannot have Christ as our Savior if we refuse to acknowledge him as our Lord. To do so is to invite God's judgment.

Matthew's two other changes say the same thing. However, these changes are hard to see in some translations. I believe Matthew changed the spelling of two names on purpose, but the the people translating the New International Version (NIV) assumed it was an honest mistake and translated it away. So when the NIV says "Abijah was the father of Asa" (Mt. 1:7), most of the best manuscripts actually say "Asaph." Historically, King Asa was the son of King Abijah, so the NIV translated it as Asa. Where the NIV says "Manasseh was the father of Amon" (1:10), most of the best manuscripts say "Amos." Same situation: King Amon was the son of King Manasseh. It is one letter different for each, but not an easy mistake to make. It would be like spelling Nixon and Jackson wrong on a list of presidents.

Instead of being mistakes, I think the changes were intentional. Asa was a king, but Asaph is one of the primary writers of the psalms after David. Through the period of the kings, the people repeatedly walked away from exclusive worship of God and it was the psalmists, Asaph and his inheritors, who called the people back to the LORD. Occasionally, they listened, but often they did not. The inclusion of Asaph in the genealogy is a reminder of God's continual call to return to worship, to return to praising him alone, to turn from idols and serve the living God. Israel's refusal to listen to the likes of Asaph was one of the reasons God brought about the exile.

Amos, on the other hand, was a prophet of God. He was most well known for criticizing Israel for its treatment of the poor. In the time of Amos, people had all the right worship services, but they trampled the poor in order to build fine houses for themselves (Amos 2:6ff.). They crushed the weak to provide safety and success for themselves. Amos promised God's judgment would remove them from the land. In short, he promised exile.

God's mercy is wide and deep, but so is his call to discipleship. The God who forgives and claims sinners and outsiders, also claims every square inch of our lives and demands that we treat the poor, the widow, the orphan, and the alien with mercy and compassion.

The gospel includes incredible forgiveness and incredible demands. It is rich with mercy and judgment. Both are part of the gospel, both are part of Jesus' genealogy, and both need to be heard in order to respond faithfully.

God's Faithfulness

The last third of the genealogy of Jesus, from the exile to Joseph, reveals God's faithfulness by bringing the Messiah out of obscurity. We already touched on this point above, but after the exile, the line of David was a joke. One major power after another had control of the land of Israel and there was no king on the throne. After Zerubbabel, most of the people named in this section are found nowhere else in Scripture. The line of David was weak, the people of Abraham oppressed, and there seemed little that could be done. Yet, God was faithful. Out of this obscure corner of an obscure family, God brought redemption. It is only God's faithfulness that can bring us through to the end.

God is faithful. The end of this genealogy is the miracle of the Messiah. Through his abundant mercy and searing judgment, God remains faithful. The promises are fulfilled. There is, finally, a seed of Abraham that will bless all the nations. There is Jesus Christ, the Savior of all the world. There is, finally, a king who will sit on David's throne forever. There is Jesus Christ, the King of kings and Lord of lords.

Matthew ends by highlighting the symmetry of God's work in bringing forth Jesus the Messiah. Fourteen generations from Abraham to David, fourteen from David to the exile to Babylon, and fourteen from the exile to the Messiah. The symmetry tells of the sovereignty of God. All along, God has been the Lord of history. For over 42 generations, the people waited and wondered and hoped. At times it seemed like all was lost, but it was never outside of God's control. The journey up to David, down to the exile, and in humility to the Messiah, all of it was part of God's sovereign plan to bring about the redemption of the world.

Conclusion

The genealogy of Jesus helps the church breathe with both lungs. It draws together the Old and New Testaments into one book proclaiming the saving work of God in Christ Jesus. This genealogy sits at the beginning of the New Testament, but connects deeply with the Old Testament.

The genealogy holds forth Jesus as the fulfillment of all God's promises in the Old Testament: Messiah, Son of Abraham, Son of David. The genealogy also holds forth the mercy, judgment, and faithfulness of God that find their fulfillment in Jesus. Through this list of names – who is included, excluded, or even intentionally misspelled – God shows how all of Scripture comes together in Jesus.

Discussion Questions:

1. How can the genealogy of Jesus help us see better the connections between the Old and New Testaments? Why is that important for our faith?

2. How do the titles used for Jesus connect with the genealogy to reveal who Jesus is? Which title speaks most to you right now — Son of Abraham, Son of David, or Messiah?

3. What does the structure of Jesus' genealogy reveal about the character of God?

Reading Backwards:

Luke 3:23-38

Then beginning with all the prophets, he interpreted to them the things about himself in all the scriptures. – Luke 24:27

It is almost impossible to read Luke's genealogy of Jesus without also considering the shape and content of the genealogy in the gospel of Matthew. Both trace the ancestry of Jesus as the legal son of Joseph and declare him a son of David and son of Abraham. Both occur early in the gospel accounts, before the public ministry of Jesus. In short, Matthew and Luke fundamentally agree on the genealogy of Jesus. There is no competition or contradiction between the two passages.

However, though they cover the same material, the two genealogies are doing different things. As we look closely at Jesus' genealogy in Luke, we will also frequently reference Matthew. The slight differences between the genealogies highlight the different ways the Spirit uses this same genealogy in the different gospels. In this chapter, we will examine the significance of the seventy-seven generations

Luke lists in the genealogy of Jesus, work to understand why some names are different between Matthew and Luke, before diving deep into the significance of the ending of Luke's genealogy. We will then step back to look at the genealogy in light of its place in the gospel. Lastly, we will consider just what kind of genealogy we have in Luke and how that might help us to read it more faithfully.

The Fullness of Time

Luke lists seventy-seven generations between Adam and Jesus. Matthew lists three sets of fourteen generations (totaling forty-two) between Abraham and Jesus. In both cases, they are using significant numbers within the context of the Bible in order to communicate something about Jesus. In the gospel of Luke, seventy-seven is meant to communicate that Jesus came in the fullness of time. Seventy is a number of fullness, as is seven. In seven days God completed the creation of the world. In Genesis 10, the list of the nations that fill the earth after the flood is numbered at seventy. The number of descendants of Jacob who traveled down to Egypt during the days of Joseph was numbered at seventy (Gen 46:27). Both numbers are a full or complete number in the Bible. Seventy-seven as the combination of the seventy (fullness of the nations and/or nation of Israel) and seven (fullness of creation) communicates an overwhelming fullness. So, when Luke records the genealogy of Jesus as having seventy-seven generations between Adam and Jesus, it was a different way of saying exactly what Paul says in Galatians: "In the fullness of time, God sent his son" (Gal 4:4). The timing of Christ's coming is intentional and perfect.

For many in the modern west, our primary concern with a genealogy is accuracy. Is it correct? Are these exact people in this exact order in a genealogy factual true in terms of history? While accuracy was important in the ancient world, the genealogies in the Bible are as much about theology as accuracy. Matthew does not simply list forty-two names, but groups them into three categories of fourteen to communicate that Jesus is the son of David, the son of Abraham, the Messiah. Luke has seventy-seven generations not only for accuracy, but for theology. Jesus came in the fullness of time.

This concern for theology as well as accuracy can help us make sense of some confusing differences between the two genealogies. Many of the same names appear in key places in both genealogies, but there are also differences. In Matthew, Jacob is the father of Joseph the husband of Mary (Mt. 1:16), but in Luke, Joseph is the son of Heli (Lk 3:23). The line between David and Zerubabbel is different in the two genealogies, as is the line from Zerubbabel to Joseph. In some instances, this may be that the same person could go by multiple names (I.e., Simon Peter, Saul and Paul), where in others the family tree might have been traced through a different ancestor. When we are looking at seventy-seven generations, there are likely multiple ways to trace the same family line. However, it is also true that not every name is listed in a genealogy. The point of a biblical genealogy is not always to be exhaustive. It was not uncommon for someone to be listed as a "son of X" or "father of Y" when there are a couple generations between them. While that might cause us to scratch our heads, this was not considered being inaccurate in the ancient world. "Son of" and "Father of" are sometimes about lineage, not direct father-son relationships. Thus, it is possible that either Luke or Matthew "skipped" generations in recording their genealogies in order to communicate a more important theological point or that they were drawing from different records that would have traced the same family back through different (complementary, not contradictory) ancestors.

Son of Adam, Son of God: The Identity of Jesus in Luke's Genealogy

Both genealogies set out to declare Jesus' identity. They connect him as a legal descendant of key covenant figures like Zerubbabel, David, Judah, Jacob, Isaac, and Abraham. But even as they do this, they have another theological point to make. For Luke, we see this both in the number of generations (seventy-seven — the fullness of time), but also in the final two names: "son of Adam, son of God" (Lk 3:38). Matthew declares Jesus as the son of David and son of Abraham, the fulfillment of all God's promises to Israel. Luke declares Jesus as son of Adam, son of God – the fulfillment of God's promise to redeem the whole world — the God-man Jesus Christ come to save.

The most striking difference between the two genealogies is that Matthew traces back to Abraham, but Luke goes all the way back to Adam. This demonstrates the breadth of Jesus' mission. While the whole of Scripture proclaims it, Luke's genealogy puts Jesus' connection to Adam front and center.

It was through Adam that sin entered the world and it is to Adam that all members of the human race are connected. In tracing Jesus back to Adam, Luke emphasizes Jesus connection to all of humanity, not simply Israel. It also draws us back to the promise of Genesis 3:15 — that a child of Eve would one day crush the head of the serpent, but would have his heel struck as well. Jesus is the fulfillment not only of the promises to Abraham, Isaac, and Jacob, to

David and Zerubbabel, but to Adam and Eve. He is the promised child. He is the second Adam. As Paul says, "For if, by the trespass of the one man, death reigned through that one man, how much more will those who receive God's abundant provision of grace and of the gift of righteousness reign in life through the one man, Jesus Christ!" (Romans 5:17). Jesus brings salvation not only to Israel, but to the whole world.

However, Jesus' genealogy traces back not just to Adam, but the genealogy ends with God. In some limited sense, Adam could be called a son of God, since God created all humanity in his image. We can possibly speak of God as the "father of the human race." In a deeper sense, all those who belong to Jesus Christ through faith are called "sons and daughters of God" through adoption. However, in the truest sense, there is only one Son of God. There is only one who was not created, but is God himself, the second person of the Trinity. "In the beginning was the Word, and the Word was with God, and the Word was God" (John 1:1).

There is a double meaning in these concluding phrases of this genealogy. What was true as a shadow in Adam is true in its fullness in Jesus Christ — the second Adam. Jesus is fully a son of Adam — fully human, like us in every way apart from sin. Jesus is also the full, true, and only Son of God — fully God, God from God, light from light, true God from true God, begotten not made, of the same essence as the Father.

The conclusion of Luke's genealogy is a bold theological statement about the identity of Jesus. He is the son of Adam and son of God. In light of the whole witness of Scripture, we can see this as a claim about Jesus as fully God and fully human — the incarnate Son of God. As son of Adam, Jesus is the second Adam who reverses the fall into sin through his life, death, and resurrection. By connecting back to Adam, Luke proclaims that the salvation that Jesus brings spreads "far as the curse is found."

The Placement of the Genealogy in the Gospel of Luke

As we have seen with other biblical genealogies, it is not only the content of the genealogy itself, but its placement in the Bible that helps us understand how to read it well. The subtle differences between Matthew and Luke's placement of the genealogy of Jesus is significant. For Matthew, the genealogy is placed at the front. It serves as a sinew connecting the Old Testament and New Testament together. The genealogy emphasizes Jesus as the fulfillment of God's promises of a Savior, Lord, and Messiah. Jesus is explicitly connected to the people of Israel and the promises and hopes of Israel through the genealogy.

However, in the gospel of Luke, the same purpose is accomplished in a different way. Zechariah and Elizabeth are like barren Israel awaiting the birth of the Messiah, earnestly and hopefully praying in the temple for deliverance. In Luke, John the Baptist's birth is the bridge between the Old Testament prophets and their fulfillment in Jesus Christ. Simeon and Anna are also like expectant Israel waiting for the Messiah to be born, rejoicing at his coming. The first three chapters of Luke make strong connections to Jesus as the fulfillment of Israel and connect him to the promises of God in the Old Testament. This frees up the genealogy in Luke to have a different function. Why would Luke place the genealogy here? Instead of a sinew connecting to the Old Testament, Luke's record of Jesus' family is a sinew connecting to the world.

The genealogy in Luke comes on the heels of Jesus'

baptism in the Jordan and before he heads to the wilderness to be tempted by the devil. The last words we hear before the beginning of the genealogy are the words of the Father pronounced over Jesus at his baptism: "You are my Son, the Beloved; with you I am well pleased." (3:22). Who is this Son, the Beloved? We already know that he is the fulfillment of the promises of God. We heard that in the angel's words to Mary, to Zechariah and Elizabeth, the pronouncements of Simeon and the praise of Anna. The genealogy answer the question about the identity of Jesus: As the son of Adam, son of God, his work is as wide as the world. Before he enters into public ministry, Luke uses the genealogy as a point to pause and direct us to the wide scope of the work of Jesus.

A Narrow Expanse: The Structure of Luke's Genealogy

All the way back when we considered Genesis 10 and 11, we noted that there are two main patterns for genealogies in the Bible: narrowing and expansion. Expansion genealogies begin with a single person or couple and show the family growing and expanding through the generations. One person becomes a people. It is a fulfillment of God's promise to fill the earth or the nation with people. It emphasizes connection, so that these various people and various groups are actually connected together. Narrowing genealogies, on the other hand, trace the fulfillment of God's covenantal promises from one generation to the other. Not everyone is named, but only those who carry on the promise. The power of the expanding genealogy is seen in where it begins — the person who is the fount of this new family. The power of the narrowing genealogy is at the end — the person who is the result of God's kept promises. Both kinds of genealogies are found throughout Scripture and both find their culmination in the genealogy of Jesus.

Matthew's genealogy is a straightforward narrowing genealogy. It begin with Abraham and shows God's faithful bringing forward of the covenant promises through David, through the exile, and all the way to Jesus. The power of the genealogy is that, at the end of all God's promise keeping, is Jesus. He stands as the great final fulfillment of the promise of the child of Eve who will crush the serpent's head. He is the one in whom all the nations of the earth will be blessed. He is the king who will reign on the throne of David forever. This is, in part, why it forms such a powerful bridge between the Old and New Testaments. It shows that, from one generation to the next, God has been faithfully keeping his covenant and that it has all led to the birth of the Messiah, Jesus.

Luke's genealogy has elements of both patterns. Its purpose is fulfillment — Jesus as the second Adam — and connection — pointing toward the salvation of the Gentiles. Jesus at the beginning is the key figure, but there is also incredible power at the end of the genealogy — son of Adam, son of God. Strictly looking at the form, we might say that Luke 3 is a narrowing genealogy, since it does not expand to show many children, but shows the coming of Jesus from one generation to the next. However, it is the only major genealogy in the Bible that works backward. The genealogy of the temple musicians in 1 Chronicles 6:33-47 also works backwards, but, whether expanding or narrowing, the genealogies of the Bible tend to move forward in time. They move from Abraham to David, not from David backward to Abraham. So Matthew records: "and Aram the father of Aminadab, and Aminadab the father of Nashon, and Nashon the father of Salmon" (Matthew 1:4). It begins in the past and moves forward in the story into the present. Yet, Luke moves in the other direction. Jesus, who is the last person in the genealogy chronologically, is listed first. Luke moves from the present back into the past. The genealogy of Luke invites us to read history backwards in light of Jesus.

Reading Backwards: Ingrafting in the Genealogy of Luke

Jesus is not only the conclusion and fulfillment of the Old Testament, but we can now look back and read the whole history of Israel differently in light of Jesus. The birth of Jesus works forward and backward. In Matthew, the genealogy connects the Old Testament forward into the person and work of Jesus. In Luke, the reversal of the form of the genealogy shows that, in Jesus, we are connected backward into the whole covenantal life with God, stretching all the way back to the Garden. Jesus Christ is the center of history. Whichever way we read — backwards or forwards — we find Jesus as the key figure in the history of the world.

These two directions may have been especially valuable based upon the original audience of the gospel. If, as some suggest, Matthew was written to a predominantly Jewish audience, it would have been incredibly valuable for them to see that the people of God — to whom they belonged — find their fulfillment in Jesus. If in Luke, as some suggest, the original audience may have been more Gentile, the connection backward would have been powerful. They had come from outside the covenant to believe in the Messiah, Jesus. Yet in Jesus, they are connected backward (grafted – to use Paul's language in Romans 9-11) into the whole covenantal history of the people of God. Those inside the covenant need to hear the genealogy in Matthew, where Jesus is the fulfillment of all God's promises made to them throughout the ages. Those born outside the convent need to hear the genealogy in Luke and learn that through faith in Christ they have been joined backward into the whole of the biblical story. Luke's readers see the genealogy of Jesus and learn that, in Jesus Christ, the whole story is now their story.

Conclusion

This call to read history backward in light of the coming of Christ comes from Jesus. It is not only found in his genealogy at the beginning of Luke, but on the lips of Jesus after his resurrection. On that first Easter Sunday, the women had encountered the angels at the empty tomb and ran, relaying the message to the gathered, trembling disciples. They were astounded, but many struggled to believe. Later that day, two of the disciples were heading to a village called Emmaus when, suddenly, Jesus began to walk alongside them. They were kept from recognizing him, but they discussed with him the tragic, surprising, and confusing events of the last few days. After telling that the women had reported the tomb empty and the appearance of the angels, Jesus said to them:

"Oh, how foolish you are, and how slow of heart to believe all that the prophets have declared! Was it not necessary that the Messiah should suffer these things and then enter into his glory?" Then beginning with all the prophets, he interpreted to them the things about himself in all the scriptures." (Luke 24:25-27)

Jesus reads the scriptures forward and backward on the road to Emmaus and it always points to him. The prophets had declared what would happen to Jesus — his death and resurrection. Reading forward, Jesus points to his work as the fulfillment of the promises of the prophets. Yet, then Jesus then opens the scriptures to them and helps them see all the things about himself in the Scriptures. He reads backwards — opening up the whole of the Bible in light of who he is and what he has done.

The two genealogies of Jesus in Matthew and Luke share in how Jesus reads the Bible. In Matthew, the genealogy moves us forward from the powerful promises of the Old Testament into the fulfillment of the New Testament. In Luke, the amazing, expansive grace of the New Testament pulls us back to re-read the Old Testament in light of the fullness of Jesus.

The genealogies serve as the sinews of Scripture. They connect the past, present, and future together in the biblical story. Nowhere is this seen more clearly than in the genealogy of Jesus. Jesus connects us, through David and Jacob and Abraham, all the way back to Adam. Yet, in Jesus, we find the fulfillment of all the promises of God, all the genealogies of scripture, all the hopes of God's people throughout the ages. The past meets its fulfillment in Jesus. Perhaps reading biblical genealogies will help us as we become better readers, not just of the genealogies, but of the whole of Scripture.

Discussion Questions:

1. "The genealogies in the Bible are as much about theology as accuracy." How does this help explain some of the differences between Matthew and Luke's genealogy? Do you find this explanation convincing?

2. Why is the way Luke's genealogy ends significant? What does it say about who Jesus is?

3. How do the different structures of Matthew and Luke's genealogy point to their different purposes and (potentially) different audiences?

4. What will be your biggest takeaway from studying these genealogies?

Conclusion:

Three Key Questions for Every Genealogy

Biblical genealogies do not have to be intimidating. Throughout *The Sinews of Scripture*, we have looked at eight different passages containing biblical genealogies in order to better understand and better equip ourselves to read any genealogy in the Bible. Each of these genealogies is unique, but there are consistent patterns that help us read them well. When we remember the three main purposes of genealogies, we can learn to ask three key questions whenever we encounter a biblical genealogy.

Purposes of Genealogies

There are three overlapping purposes of genealogies in the Bible. First, genealogies remind us that the Bible is a family story. Just as you might read a genealogy of your family in order to look for where one of your ancestors connects with an old family story, the people of Israel would read the genealogies and find themselves in the story. They knew their clan, their tribe, their family, and would see themselves caught up in the story as they read the genealogies.

Second, genealogies show God keeping his promises as the people awaited the birth of *the* child. God promised a child of Eve who would crush the head of the serpent. He promised Abram that from his seed God would bless all the nations of the earth. He promised David that he would have a son who would reign on the throne forever. With every generation in a genealogy was the lingering question, "Is this the child?" The search for children and the crisis of barrenness was not only personal, but wrapped up in God's promised redemption. The genealogies help carry forward the covenantal promises even as the people waited for the coming of Jesus.

Lastly, genealogies serve as the connective tissue of Scripture. They connect the past, present, and future of the biblical story together. They bridge what came before to what will come. Sometimes this connection is strictly chronological, but it is often theological as well. Through their specific details, the genealogies help us to see the past and future in light of one another. We saw how Esau's genealogy helped us see deeper connections to the persons of Lot and Saul. We saw how the structure of Jesus' genealogy in Matthew and Luke spoke of Jesus' identity and mission. Far from being random interludes in the main story, the genealogies serves as the connective tissue that helps hold the whole of Scripture together into a coherent whole. The genealogies connect and thus remind us that whatever individual story or book we are reading, this is all one story, one book, that speaks with one voice.

Conclusion

Key Questions for Reading Genealogies

As we worked our way through eight different passages containing genealogies we have noticed several consistent patterns that flesh out those main purposes of genealogies. First, we saw that genealogies tend to have one of two patterns: narrowing and expansion. Expansion genealogies start with an individual or couple and expand to include all of their descendants. The important piece of the genealogy is the beginning, the head of the family. These genealogies emphasize the connection between various people and groups of people and God's faithfulness to fill the earth and fill the nation with people. Narrowing genealogies are more closely tied to God's fulfillment of his covenant promises. They touch more closely on the question, "Is this the child?" In these genealogies, the family is traced through one son after another, with the most important person being at the end of the genealogy. Usually, this person is the next key figure who will carry forward the covenant of God (e.g. Abraham, David, Jesus). One of the key skills in reading any genealogy will be identifying whether it is a narrowing or expansion genealogy, because this form helps us better understand the reason it was included in the Bible and how we should read it. In short, we should ask **"Who is this genealogy telling us about?"** as we approach reading genealogies. Expansion genealogies tell us about the person at the beginning, while narrowing genealogies focus on the person at the end.

Second, we saw repeatedly that the genealogies found their fulfillment in Jesus Christ. This should not be surprising, since the whole of Scripture points to Jesus, but we have seen that this is specifically true of the biblical genealogies. **"How does this genealogy point to Jesus?"** will be another key question for reading any genealogy.

Third, the placement of a genealogy within the larger context of Scripture is crucial for understanding it profitably. The placement of Matthew and Luke's genealogies are intentional and tell us a lot about what they are doing in the book. Ruth's genealogy at the end serves as the powerful punchline of the whole book, with her gracious inclusion in the people of God being tied into the larger story of God's salvation. **"Why is this genealogy here?"** will be a third key question for reading further genealogies.

With these three questions in hand and all that we have learned through the genealogies we explored, you should be better prepared to read any of the genealogies we did not cover in this handbook.

OTHER GENEALOGIES

As we close, I want to take a brief look at a few of the genealogies we did not cover in this book and suggest how what we learned might apply in reading them.

1 Chronicles: This book opens with an expansion genealogy that covers much of the early genealogies from Genesis word for word. Much of what we discussed in exploring those genealogies would apply for Chronicles, though many of the specific details from Genesis are not included in 1 Chronicles. The genealogy continues more specifically into the line of Judah and David, as well as Benjamin and Saul. There are two main differences to consider. First, we should pay attention to the overall placement of the genealogy within the book of 1 Chronicles and what that might communicate. Second, we should ask why such an extensive genealogy was considered important enough for us to know that it would take up nine whole chapters.

1-2 Kings: These are not strictly genealogies, but they narrate the various kings of Israel and Judah. However, they do run somewhat closely in form to a narrowing genealogy, with the overall purpose being the search for the Son of David, who will reign in righteousness. We see this particularly in how all the kings are judged by the standard of David himself. Thus, 1-2 Kings shows the repeated failure of the kings to live into this covenantal calling and the slow, spiraling descent of the nation into sin, destruction, and exile.

Ezra: The genealogies here are expansion genealogies that record the people who returned from exile and resettled in the land. Their placement within the book will be important to consider as well as how God's refilling of the land with people (however small in number) shows forth his faithfulness and grace to his people.

The genealogies in the Bible do not have to be intimidating. Not only do they hold the Bible together, but they can also serve to build up our faith. My hope has been that, through this book, you will have grown in confidence and even excitement about what God might teach you through the genealogies of the Bible.

For Further Reading

At the beginning of the book, I said that there is value in technical expertise. We need books that use extensive language and cultural study. I have personally benefited from many of these books. Below are a few of those books to help you on your journey of growing as a reading of Scripture:

On Reading Scripture Well

Alastair Roberts and Andrew Wilson, *Echoes of Exodus: Tracing Themes of Redemption through Scripture*. Crossway: Wheaton, IL, 2018.

Augustine, *On Christian Teaching*, translated by R. P. H. Green. Oxford University Press: Oxford, 1997.

John Calvin, *Calvin's Commentaries*, 22 volumes. Baker Books: Grand Rapids, 2009.

John Calvin, *Institutes of the Christian Religion*, 2 Volumes. Edited by John T. McNeill, translated by Ford Lewis Battles. Library of Christian Classics, Volume XX. Westminster Press: Philadelphia, 1960. I.VI-VIII.

Richard A. Muller, *Post-Reformation Reformed Dogmatics: The Rise and Development of Reformed Orthodoxy, ca. 1520 to ca. 1725, Volume Two: Holy Scripture, the Cognitive Foundation of Theology*, Second Edition. Baker Academic: Grand Rapids, 2003.

Eugene Peterson, *Eat This Book: A Conversation in the Art of Spiritual Reading*. Eerdmans: Grand Rapids, 2006.

Lois Tverberg, *Reading the Bible with Rabbi Jesus: How a Jewish Perspective Can Transform Your Understanding*. Baker Books: Grand Rapids, 2017.

On Genesis

Nahum M. Sarna, *Understanding Genesis: The Heritage of Biblical Israel*. Schocken Books: New York, 1966.

R. R. Reno, *Genesis*. Brazos Theological Commentary on

the Bible. Brazos Press: Grand Rapids, MI, 2010.

Sidney Greidanus, *Preaching Christ from Genesis: Foundations for Expository Sermons*. Eerdmans: Grand Rapids, MI, 2007.

On Matthew

F. Dale Bruner, *Matthew: A Commentary*. 2 Volumes. Eerdmans: Grand Rapids, MI, 2004.

Craig S. Keener, *The Gospel of Matthew: A Socio-Rhetorical Commentary*, Eerdmans: Grand Rapids, MI, 2009.

Acknowledgements

Behind each individual project is a group of people who gave of their time and energy along the way. I want to offer a special thank you to Pamela Bos, Susan Denny, Juanita Eveleigh, Anja Noordam, Olga Shaffer, and Terri Wing, who read early versions of these chapters and provided feedback. Your contributions made this book significantly better.

For Bethel Reformed Church, thank you for your love and support these past years. Thank you for bearing witness to the breadth and depth of the mercy of Jesus.

For Olga, thank you for all that you do to make books like this possible. I cannot name the number of roles you filled in this process. You were a mother, wife, cover designer, proofreader, beta-reader, typesetter, and sounding board – just to name a few. This book is as much your creation as it is mine.

For Elijah, Moriah, and Joanna, thank you for loving Jesus, loving books, and loving your Daddy as he writes books. You are always in my heart and on my mind as I write.

Also by
Stephen C. Shaffer

Our Only Comfort: Daily Devotions through the Heidelberg Catechism

In a fast-paced world full of distractions, how do we create space to have conversations about faith? Parents long to talk about Jesus with their children, but are unsure where to begin. Families want to slow down and reconnect with what matters most, but struggle to squeeze anything into already busy schedules. Teens and adults desire to go deeper in their faith, but are filled with unanswered questions. In *Our Only Comfort*, Rev. Stephen Shaffer provides individuals and families with a helpful structure for growing in Christian faith. In a series of 364 devotions, *Our Only Comfort* will take families, young adults, and new believers through the core teachings of the Christian faith through the lens of the Heidelberg Catechism. Wrestling through questions like "Who is Jesus?" "How do I pray?" and "What does it mean to keep the Ten Commandments?" these short devotions create opportunity for conversations about faith between parents and children and provide nourishment for faith to grow.

Paperback: 978-1725298736
Hardcover: 978-1725298743

All Things Hold Together: Recovering Christian Worldview

In Christ, all things hold together. Apart from him, things fall apart. The multitude of fractures in our world result from the removal of our center in Christ. Worldview is not a weapon. It was meant to mend the fractures opened up by the modern world. The recovery of a theological center, of a Christian worldview, serves as a way to sew back together what the modern world seeks to rip apart. Worldview gives voice to a way before and beyond the fractures, a world we have abandoned in order to rule ourselves.

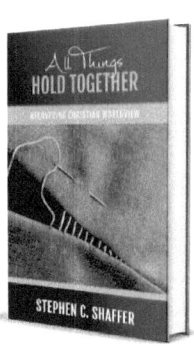

Paperback: 978-1777978761
Hardcover: 978-1777978754

Rooted: Growing in Christ in a Rootless Age

In a rootless world, we long for a place where we find peace, rest, and belonging.

The soil of our society is not particularly well-suited for growing deep roots of character and Christian identity. The consistent pattern of uprooting our lives and families for a new job, a new opportunity, a new church has left our roots damaged, our friendships weak, and our souls drained. We long for a place where we are known, loved, and even challenged to live more fully.

The longing for home, for place, for rootedness is ultimately a longing for Jesus. Wrestling with the biblical themes of land and exile, *Rooted: Growing in Christ in a Rootless Age* is a call to grow more at home in our true home, Jesus Christ. Walking along with Israel from Eden through the Exodus to the Exile, Stephen C. Shaffer shows how God both rooted and uprooted his people so that they would find their identity and center in God.

Paperback: 978-1777978709
Hardcover: 978-1777978716

www.ingramcontent.com/pod-product-compliance
Lightning Source LLC
Chambersburg PA
CBHW060611080526
44585CB00013B/778